Practice Test #1

1. Of the following expenses incurred in the construction, which are hard costs? (choose 2)
   a. Concrete
   b. Architecture fees
   c. Concrete contractor's fee
   d. Construction insurance

2. In order to be eligible to become a LEED AP, a candidate MUST do all of the following, EXCEPT:
   a. Provide a letter of attestation
   b. Agree to the credential maintenance requirements
   c. Have previous experience with a LEED Registered Project within three years of the date the application is submitted
   d. Be currently involved in a LEED Registered Project

3. Which categories are common to most LEED rating systems? (choose 3)
   a. Sustainable Sites
   b. Exemplary Performance
   c. Energy and Atmosphere
   d. Water Efficiency

4. What are some of the benefits of green buildings? (choose 3)
   a. They minimize the human use of limited natural resources.
   b. They generate less waste.
   c. They allow for a decrease in landscaping.
   d. They increase human productivity.

5. What is the EIA?
   a. Energy Input Alliance
   b. Environmental Information Administration
   c. Energy Information Administration
   d. None of the above

6. How can the Commercial Buildings Energy Consumption Survey (CBECS) be used?
   a. To determine how much energy a solar panel puts out
   b. To determine estimated electricity use in commercial buildings
   c. To determine estimated energy use in homes
   d. To determine estimated energy output for commercial buildings

7. Life-cycle assessment encompasses all of the following, EXCEPT:
   a. Design
   b. Operations
   c. Waste
   d. Renewal

8. What are the purposes of life-cycle cost analysis? (choose 2)
   a. To identify which high performance building systems will save money over the life of the project
   b. To compare different designs and identify which one represents the best long-term investment
   c. To determine the least expensive construction method
   d. To identify which construction materials are the most resilient

9. Which of the following are examples of an integrative approach? (choose 2)
   a. The owner purchases a site and then hires an architect to design the building.
   b. A team consisting of the owner, architects, planners, engineers, and other professionals is assembled to map out a project.
   c. An architect designs a building and then hands it off to a landscape architect and civil and mechanical engineers to design their pieces of the building.
   d. A project includes specifying a more expensive, high performance window that could allow for the use of a smaller, less expensive HVAC system.

10. A study done by the New Buildings Institute found that, in green buildings, average energy use intensity (energy consumed per unit of floor space) is how much lower than in typical buildings?
    a. 12%
    b. 24%
    c. 10%
    d. 40%

11. All the following are true of green buildings, EXCEPT:
    a. The average cost of a green building is between 2 and 5% more than a conventional building.
    b. Green-certified buildings do not command higher rents.
    c. They result in a 2–16% increase in student and worker performance.
    d. LEED Gold certified buildings have the best overall performance.

12. Which are components of LEED's "triple bottom line" approach?
    a. Building, resources, and pollution
    b. Building, landscape, and pollution
    c. Society, building, and resources
    d. Society, environment, and economy

13. Which is NOT a responsibility of the Green Building Certification Institute (GCBI)?
    a. To manage all aspects of the LEED Professional Accreditation program
    b. To oversee the development and maintenance program for LEED APs
    c. To develop new accreditation procedures for LEED certification
    d. To establish continuing education programs for LEED APs

14. Which of the following is NOT a LEED rating system?
    a. LEED for New Construction
    b. LEED for Hospitals
    c. LEED for Retail
    d. LEED for Existing Buildings Operations & Maintenance

15. A project team has identified that it can earn 51 points toward LEED Silver Certification. What is the minimum number of additional points required for the project to earn LEED Gold Certification?
   a. 9 points
   b. 7 points
   c. 8 points
   d. 12 points

16. Credit weights emphasize all of the following, EXCEPT:
   a. Energy efficiency
   b. Renewable energy
   c. Water conservation
   d. Recycling

17. The Wingspread Principles calls for a reduction of green house gas emissions by what percentage below the 1990 level by mid-century?
   a. 10–20%
   b. 20–40%
   c. 50–60%
   d. 60–80%

18. Which of the following contributes to a building's carbon footprint? (choose 2)
   a. The per-occupant ratio of trash production
   b. Energy used by building systems
   c. Building-related transportation
   d. Inefficient windows

19. The application fee for LEED certification is based upon which of the following?
   a. The level of certification (Certified, Silver, Gold, Platinum)
   b. The square footage of the project
   c. The footprint of the project
   d. The environmental significance of the project

20. What is the purpose of the Credit Interpretation Request (CIR)?
   a. It allows project applicants to seek technical and administrative guidance on how specific credits apply to their project.
   b. It offers project teams ideas on how to achieve a specific credit.
   c. It is a forum for a project team to ask the USGBC and other professionals design-related questions.
   d. None of the above

21. The sustainability of a project site is the sum of which of the following? (choose 3)
   a. Transportation
   b. Site design and management
   c. Stormwater management
   d. Native planting

22. Which of the following locations would qualify as a sustainable site? (choose 2)
    a. A former gas station
    b. 1 acre in an animal preserve
    c. A deserted building in a downtown area
    d. 20 acres of prime farmland

23. What is the result of increasing the demand for building materials that have been regionally extracted, processed, and manufactured?
    a. It discourages nationwide manufacturing.
    b. It supports the use of indigenous resources and reduces the environmental impacts of transportation.
    c. It reduces the availability of construction materials nationally.
    d. None of the above.

24. Transportation accounted for 32% of total U.S. green house gas emissions in 2007. Which of the following are strategies for reducing transportation? (choose 3)
    a. Riding bikes
    b. Using a carpool
    c. Providing more free parking
    d. Using public transportation

25. A renovated office building is near public transportation. What can the project team do to encourage workers to use public transportation? (choose 3)
    a. Provide a gas allowance
    b. Provide a shuttle service from the building to public transportation
    c. Provide a ride board
    d. Subsidize bus passes

26. Which of the following contribute to greenhouse gas emissions from transportation? (choose 3)
    a. Vehicle technology
    b. Electricity production
    c. Transportation fuels
    d. Land use

27. Why does LEED for Neighborhood Development encourage development within and near existing communities or public transportation? (choose 2)
    a. To reduce the need for carpools
    b. To reduce miles traveled
    c. To support walking as a transportation choice
    d. To encourage the installation pay parking lots

28. "Real property, the expansion, redevelopment, or reuse of which may be complicated by the presence or potential presence of a hazardous substance, pollutant or contaminant" is the definition of:
    a. Rehabilitated sites
    b. Redeveloped sites
    c. Risk assessments
    d. Brownfields

29. All the following are strategies of sustainable landscapes, EXCEPT:
    a. Native and adapted plants
    b. More impervious area
    c. Water-efficient irrigation
    d. Reducing impact outdoor lighting

30. Impervious materials contribute to which of the following? (choose 2)
    a. Infiltration of stormwater runoff
    b. Soil erosion
    c. Sedimentation in local waterways
    d. All of the above

31. Strategies for reducing and controlling stormwater runoff include: (choose 3)
    a. Harvesting rainwater
    b. Building projects with larger footprints
    c. Vegetated roofs
    d. Increasing pervious materials

32. What is the term used by the EPA for stormwater runoff with entrained contaminants carried into rivers and streams?
    a. Flood water
    b. Contaminated water
    c. Nonpoint source pollution
    d. Localized pollution

33. The three categories of water use are: (choose 3)
    a. Indoor water
    b. Outdoor water
    c. Process water
    d. Sanitary water

34. Municipally-supplied water is America's primary source water for domestic, commercial, and industrial use. What is this water called?
    a. Well water
    b. Potable water
    c. Gray water
    d. Recycled water

35. Non-potable water can be used for which of the following? (choose 3)
    a. Flushing toilets
    b. Watering plants
    c. Washing clothes
    d. Cooling HVAC equipment

36. Which of the following is a result of overwhelmed wastewater treatment facilities?
    a. Slow water delivery
    b. Increased supply of water
    c. Overflow of untreated water
    d. All the above

37. Efficiency strategies, combined with submetering, can improve indoor water conservation in commercial buildings. What are some other advantages of submetering? (choose 3)
    a. Monitor water use
    b. Track fixture performance
    c. Choose irrigation systems
    d. Identify problems

38. How can indoor water use be reduced? (choose 3)
    a. Use non-potable water
    b. Install submeters
    c. Install water fountains
    d. Install efficient plumbing fixtures

39. A plumbing fixture that uses less water than specified in the Energy Policy Act of 1992 (EPAct 1992) requirements is called what?
    a. Slow-flow fixture
    b. Low-flow fixture
    c. No-flush fixture
    d. Conservation fixture

40. When accessing water usage systems, a project team should consider all the following, EXCEPT:
    a. Baseline versus design
    b. Geographical location
    c. Gallons per flush
    d. Gallons per minute

41. Which of the following irrigation systems is the least efficient?
    a. Drip
    b. Bubbler
    c. Spray
    d. Weather-based system

42. Why are native and adapted species preferred in specifying landscaping? (choose 3)
    a. They grow slowly.
    b. They can thrive with little or no irrigation.
    c. They do not require pesticides.
    d. They do not require fertilizer.

43. Which of the following is not a source for non-potable water?
    a. Harvested rain water
    b. Gray water
    c. Municipal reclaimed water
    d. Black water

44. Which of the following are examples of processed water? (choose 2)
    a. Cooling towers
    b. Irrigation
    c. Sewage conveyance
    d. Dishwashers

45. Which of the following are standards for energy efficiency? (choose 2)
    a. Green Label
    b. Energy Star
    c. ASHRAE 90.1 2004
    d. E-Score

46. What is first step toward saving energy?
    a. Reduce demand
    b. Install dimmers
    c. Install solar panels
    d. Install wind turbines

47. A design team is brainstorming strategies to save energy in a new office building. Which of the following may be some of the team's ideas? (choose 2)
    a. Orient the building to maximize shade from an adjacent building
    b. Use as much glass as possible to maximize daylight
    c. Insulate the building properly against heating and cooling losses
    d. Design a larger building that is lower to the ground

48. Reducing a building's size can have a direct impact on the building's energy demand. Which LEED rating system includes an adjustment to compensate for the effect of square footage on resource consumption by adjusting the points threshold for certification?
    a. LEED for New Construction
    b. LEED for Healthcare
    c. LEED for Homes
    d. LEED for Schools

49. Which of the following are effective strategies for achieving energy efficiency? (choose 2)
    a. Purchase E-Star appliances and equipment
    b. Implement passive design techniques
    c. Install high-performance glazing
    d. Design district heating and cooling systems to ensure that each building is run independently

50. LEED for NC requires that new buildings exceed the baseline energy performance standards established by the baseline building that complies with:
    a. ASHRAE 52.2
    b. ASHRAE 55 2004 Appendix G
    c. ASHRAE 62.1 1999 Appendix H
    d. ASHRAE 90.1 2004 Appendix G

51. Which of the following items is process energy? (choose 3)
    a. Elevators
    b. Computers
    c. Interior lights
    d. Refrigerators

52. Energy that must comply with LEED's minimum performance requirements is called:
    a. Process energy
    b. Regulated energy
    c. Green energy
    d. Primary energy

53. Which of the following has the greatest ozone depletion potential (ODP)?
    a. HCFCs
    b. HFCs
    c. CFCs
    d. GWPs

54. Renewable energy sources include: (choose 3)
    a. Solar
    b. Wind
    c. Natural gas
    d. Geothermal

55. The purpose of building commissioning is to ensure that a building's related systems are installed, are calibrated, and perform according to which of the following? (choose 2)
    a. Code requirements
    b. ASHRAE 90.1 2004
    c. The owner's requirements
    d. BOD

56. Green building addresses which problems related to materials and resources during construction? (choose 2)
    a. Waste management
    b. Environmental pollution
    c. Life cycle impacts
    d. Energy consumption

57. All of the following are material and resource strategies that are encouraged by LEED, EXCEPT:
    a. FSC-certified wood products
    b. Materials that take less than 5 years to grow or raise
    c. Waste diversion
    d. Materials that originate with 500 miles of the project site

58. A building is undergoing a major renovation. Which of the following practices are sound waste management strategies? (choose 2)
    a. Gather demolished concrete to facilitate easy hauling to the landfill
    b. Pile wood studs for disposal at a nearby incineration facility
    c. Collect windows to donate to Habitat for Humanity
    d. Set up recycling bins for workers

59. How does construction waste disposal contribute to greenhouse gas emissions? (choose 3)
   a. Decay at landfills produces methane gas.
   b. Transportation emits carbon dioxide.
   c. Decay produces CFCs.
   d. Incineration emits carbon dioxide.

60. Which of the following are sustainable product certifications recognized by LEED? (choose 3)
   a. FSC
   b. Green Seal
   c. Green Plus
   d. Green Label Plus

61. A project team plans to purchase windows with an FSC sticker from a manufacturer whose factory is 550 miles from the project site. The glass used to make the windows is from a factory 250 miles from the project site. The windows could earn points in which of the following categories?
   a. Rapidly renewable and regional materials
   b. Regional materials and sustainable forestry
   c. Sustainable forestry
   d. Regional materials

62. A project team is considering specifying materials that would qualify toward points in the rapidly renewable category. Which of the following should the team specify? (choose 3)
   a. Cotton insulation
   b. Walnut doors
   c. Bamboo flooring
   d. Wool carpet

63. Which of the following would not count toward points in the reuse category? (choose 2)
   a. Recycled copper plumbing pipe
   b. Light fixtures from an antique supplier
   c. Bathroom exhaust fans
   d. Windows from a salvage yard

64. Which of the following are tools that can help project teams conduct life cycle assessments associated with a product, process, or service? (choose 2)
   a. EPEAT
   b. DOE
   c. BEES 3.0
   d. ASHRAE 55

65. Which of the following environments has the greatest concentrations of pollutants?
   a. A park
   b. An 8-year-old house where the windows are always open
   c. A new high-rise office building
   d. A loading dock

66. Improved indoor environmental quality can do which of the following? (choose 2)
   a. Increase the resale value of the building
   b. Increase operational expenses
   c. Increase the health insurance costs of occupants
   d. Reduce the liability for building owners

67. A project team wishing to provide a healthy indoor environment and reduce building-related health problems must address which issues? (choose two)
   a. Indoor air quality
   b. Thermal comfort, lighting, and acoustics
   c. Location
   d. Neighbors

68. Which of the following are indicators of poor ventilation in buildings? (choose two)
   a. Occupants report loss of concentration
   b. Absolute concentrations greater than 800–1,000 ppm
   c. CO_2 equal to outdoor levels
   d. CO_2 concentrations greater than 500 ppm above outdoor conditions

69. A project team is researching low VOC carpets for a renovated building. The team might look for carpets carrying which seal?
   a. Green Label Plus
   b. Green Seal
   c. Green-e
   d. FSC-certified

70. MERV ratings are an assessment of which of the following?
   a. How much clean energy a photovoltaic panel emits
   b. The efficiency of air filters in a mechanical system
   c. The pollution level of storm water runoff
   d. The incremental energy savings

71. Which of the following sets thermal comfort standards?
   a. ASHRAE 62.1
   b. ASHRAE 90.1
   c. ASHRAE 52.2
   d. ASHRAE 55

72. Proper ventilation rates are prescribed by which standard?
   a. ASHRAE 62.1
   b. ASHRAE 90.1
   c. ASHRAE 52.2
   d. ASHRAE 55

73. Indoor air quality can be adversely affected by which of the following? (Choose 2)
   a. Carbon dioxide
   b. Cool outdoor air
   c. Off-gassing new furniture
   d. Paint with a GS-11 label

74. Which of the following are effective ways to control the concentration of indoor pollutants?
   a. Tightly seal all of the windows
   b. Increase ventilation
   c. Use FSC-certified wood
   d. Install Green Label Plus carpet

75. All of the following choices are strategies for maintaining indoor air quality, EXCEPT:
   a. Install filters with MERV 13 or higher rating
   b. Prohibit smoking in and around the building
   c. Provide ventilation consistent with ASHRAE 55
   d. Use green cleaning products

76. Studies have shown that occupants are more satisfied with their environments if they can do which of the following? (choose 3)
   a. Open and close window shades
   b. Open and close windows
   c. Have more privacy
   d. Have task lighting for individual work stations

77. A project team can improve thermal comfort, lighting, and acoustics in indoor environments by doing which of the following? (choose 2)
   a. Provide one master light switch
   b. Provide views to the outside
   c. Give occupants temperature control
   d. Ask vice presidents for their opinion

78. All the following are effective ways to give building occupants control over the light in their personal work space, EXCEPT.
   a. Provide a window with a shade
   b. Provide task lighting
   c. Provide a dimmer
   d. Provide color-corrected fluorescent lights

79. Which are strategies recognized by LEED for earning Innovation in Design (ID) credits? (choose 2)
   a. Exceptional design
   b. Exceptional performance
   c. Inventive design
   d. Innovation

80. How can a project team earn ID credits for exceptional performance? (choose 3)
   a. Doubling density requirements for Sustainable Sites credits
   b. Using MERV 16 filters to in Indoor Environmental Quality credits
   c. Reducing indoor water use by 60%
   d. Providing 85% daylighting

81. Innovative strategies that could earn ID credits include: (choose 2)
    a. Collecting paper from shredders for recycling
    b. Developing an educational outreach program
    c. Installing 20% more bike racks than required by LEED
    d. Incorporating high levels of fly ash in concrete

82. A new elementary school project has three LEED APs on the team. What is the maximum number of credits it can earn for their involvement in this project?
    a. 1
    b. 2
    c. 3
    d. 4

83. What international treaty was developed to protect the ozone layer by banning the production of CFCs and phasing out HCFCs?
    a. The Kyoto Protocol
    b. The Montreal Protocol
    c. The Clean Air Act
    d. ASHRAE 62

84. Which of the following are examples of off-site renewable energy? (Choose 2)
    a. RECs
    b. DOEs
    c. VOCs
    d. TRCs

85. Which of the following are benefits of a vegetated roof? (choose 2)
    a. Indicates the building is LEED-certified
    b. Reduces the heat island effect
    c. Aids in stormwater runoff quantity and quality
    d. Can help generate green power

86. Which of the following is an example of a "smart location?"
    a. 50% of dwelling units within a ½ mile walk of a bus
    b. 75% of dwelling units within ½ mile of a rail station
    c. 75% of dwelling units within 200 yards of a bike rack
    c. 50% of dwelling units within 500 yards of a carpool stop

87. What is LID?
    a. Local Intensive Development
    b. LEED Integrated Development
    c. Low Impact Development
    d. Land Integrated Development

88. A baseline versus design model is used for which of the following? (choose 2)
    a. To estimate water use savings
    b. To estimate green power need
    c. To estimate energy performance
    d. To estimate recycled materials

89. Which of the following individuals is eligible to take the LEED GA exam? (choose 2)
    a. A USGCB member
    b. Someone who has taken a USGBC course
    c. An architecture intern
    d. A former employee of a photovoltaic manufacturer

90. A project team is specifying non-FSC-certified wood panels with recycled wood for a new office building. What should the team do to earn LEED credit?
    a. The wood panels are not eligible for LEED credit
    b. List the entire wood panel
    c. List only the percentage that is recycled
    d. Replace the panels with an FSC-certified product

91. The Chain of Custody (COC) number is associated with which other certification?
    a. Green Label Plus
    b. EPEAT
    c. Green Seal
    d. FSC

92. Which of the following are LEED for Neighborhood Development credit categories? (choose 2)
    a. Sustainable Sites
    b. Water Efficiency
    c. Neighborhood Pattern and Design
    d. Green Infrastructure and Buildings

93. Who is the project team member responsible for making an appeal(s) to a final credit ruling reviewed during the Construction Review?
    a. LEED AP
    b. Project Administrator
    c. Project Leader
    d. Architect

94. How can project teams submit documentation of credit compliance?
    a. Through USGBC customer service
    b. By emailing the USGBC
    c. Through LEED-Online
    d. Through the GCBI

95. All the following are true of a footcandle EXCEPT:
    a. A footcandle is equal to one lumen per square foot
    b. A footcandle is the measure of the amount of illumination falling on a surface
    c. Minimizing the number of footcandles of site lighting helps reduce light pollution
    d. Increasing the number of footcandles is less disruptive to nocturnal animals

96. Which of the following are appropriate strategies for developing a sustainable site? (choose 2)
    a. Increasing the building footprint
    b. Using exterior surfaces that have high SRI values
    c. Using more impervious surfaces
    d. Installing irrigation systems that use gray water

97. The project team of a six-story residential project is going to pursue LEED Silver Certification. Which LEED Rating System should the team pursue?
    a. LEED for Homes
    b. LEED for Core & Shell
    c. LEED for New Construction
    d. LEED for Multi-Family

98. Which of the following will not qualify for a LEED credit point with respect to refrigerants?
    a. An existing building that has implemented a 50% phase-out of CFC-based refrigerants prior to project completion
    b. A new building that uses no refrigerants
    c. A new building that uses propane as a refrigerant
    d. a new building that uses ammonia as a refrigerant

99. A project team is studying a building's energy use patterns. Which of the following will have the least impact on energy use?
    a. Fenestration and building envelope
    b. Interior walls and partitions
    c. Roof features
    d. Building siting and landscaping

100. What is the very minimum that a project team must successfully do in order to attain LEED Certification? (choose 3)
    a. Collect documentation for all prerequisites
    b. Collect documentation for 40 points
    c. File a CIR
    d. Register with the USGBC

Answer Key and Explanations

1. A & C: Hard costs are those expenses that are directly tied to the actual construction of the building, for example, land costs, machinery, construction labor, and materials. Soft costs include architectural, engineering, financial, legal, as well as pre- and post-construction expenses.

2. D: The candidate must provide a letter from a supervisor, client, or project manager describing the candidate's role in the project. Additionally, in accordance with the USGBC requirements:
- The letter must be on letterhead or provide other evidence of its authenticity.
- The body of the attestation should be limited to 1,500 words or less.
- The letter must be dated.
- The letter must be authored and signed by a supervisor, client, project manager, or someone else who is qualified to evaluate the applicant's performance.
- The author's title and relationship to the applicant should be demonstrated, for example, include the author's business card.
- The letter must summarize and confirm the applicant's involvement with the LEED Project.
- The full name or Project ID for the LEED Project must be provided.
- The dates of the applicant's relevant involvement in the project must be noted in the letter.
- If the applicant is not currently involved with the noted LEED project, the end date of this involvement cannot be more than three (3) years ago.

    Note: 5–7 percent of letters will be audited.

3. A, C, & D: There are six categories common to all LEED products: Sustainable Sites, Water Efficiency, Energy and Atmosphere, Materials and Resources, Indoor Environmental Quality, and Innovation in Design. A seventh category, Regional Design, has been developed to address regionally-relevant issues. LEED for Homes has two additional categories: Location and Linkage and Awareness and Education. LEED for Neighborhood Development is organized into three categories: Smart Location and Linkage, Neighborhood Pattern and Design, and Green Infrastructure and Buildings. Exemplary Performance is one way to earn Innovative Design points, but it is not a category.

4. A, B, & D: Regardless of the fact that green buildings are more efficient and comfortable than non-green buildings, they also reduce human use of natural resources, lower operational costs, use less energy, generate less waste, and increase human productivity.

5. C: The EIA, or Energy Information Administration, falls under the Department of Energy (DOE). It publishes the 2003 *Commercial Sector Average Energy Costs by State*, which, as its name implies, is a resource for calculating the cost of energy by state.

6. B: CBECS is the Department of Energy's (DOE) database that can be used to determine estimated electricity use in commercial buildings. This information is the baseline from which reductions are made and alternative energy resources, such as renewable energy (EAc2) and green power (EAc6), are employed to earn LEED credits.

7. C: Life-cycle assessment begins at the inception of an idea and continues until a project reaches the end of its life and its components are recycled and reused. The analysis takes into account not just the building, but its materials and components—everything from extraction through transport and then recycling, reuse, or disposal. The intent of the life-cycle assessment is to inform the choice of building materials and systems in an effort to minimize the negative impact of construction and land use.

8. A & B: Life-cycle cost analysis is considered the costs during the entire life of the building; it takes into account both the initial costs or first costs (for example, capital and construction) and the operational costs incurred during the lifetime of the building. This allows for a full-picture illustration of the lifetime costs, including constructing and running the building (for example: costs for maintenance, repair, personnel, and utilities). This information allows the project team to identify the approach that offers the lowest overall cost of ownership.

9. A & D: An integrative approach is a collaborative process that requires all of those involved in the design and construction of the building to contribute their skills, knowledge, and expertise. It considers the building as a whole. This process is most beneficial when initiated at the conception of a project; it is often non linear and nonhierarchical. This differs from the conventional design process, which is linear and often has each profession and trade working in turns, often independent of one another.

10. B: Additionally, a U.S. General Administration survey of 12 green buildings found:
   - 13% lower maintenance costs
   - 26% less energy usage
   - 27% higher levels of occupant satisfaction
   - 33% lower CO2 emissions

11. B: The public overestimates the cost of green buildings. The World Business Council for Sustainable Development found that correspondents believed that green building features added 17% to the overall cost of construction, whereas a survey of 146 green buildings put the actual marginal increase at less than 2%. A study done by California Berkeley found that certified green office buildings rented for 2% more than comparable conventional buildings. When adjusted for occupancy levels, they found a 6% premium for certified buildings.

12. D: The term "triple bottom line" was coined by John Elkington in 1994 to shift the measurement of corporate performance from the perspective of a shareholder to that of a stakeholder in an attempt to coordinate the interests of "people, planet, and profit." The USGBC has adapted the term to establish a rating system designed to measure and recognize building projects based on their performance in each of three categories of sustainability: society, the environment, and the economy.

13. C: "Certification" is the rating process for buildings; it is administered by USGBC. GCBI is a separate, incorporated entity established in 2007 with the support of USGBC. GCBI administers credentialing programs related to the green building practice.

14. B: LEED rating systems are:
- LEED for New Construction
- LEED for Core & Shell
- LEED for Commercial Interiors
- LEED for Schools
- LEED for Healthcare
- LEED for Retail
- LEED for Existing Buildings Operations & Maintenance
- LEED for Homes
- LEED for Neighborhood Development

15. A: Achieving LEED certification requires satisfying all prerequisites and earning the minimum number of points required in the applicable rating system:
- Certified: 40–49 points
- Silver: 50–59 points
- Gold: 60–79 points
- Platinum: 80+ points

The question asks for the "minimum" number of additional points required (9); 12 points is more than the "minimum."

16. D: Credit weights give more weight to those credits within the LEED rating system that most directly address the most important environmental impacts, particularly green house gas emissions. The impact categories are defined by the U.S. EPA. The other credit weight emphasized is reduced transportation demand.

17. D: The USGB is a signatory to Wingspread Principles on a U.S. Response to Global Warming. It is signed by individuals and organizations who have declared their commitment to addressing climate change. The principles are based on the recognition that climate change is a global challenge that requires changes in our economy, policy, and behavior.

18. B & C: A building's carbon footprint is the total green house gases associated with its construction and operation. The other contributing factors are:
- Embodied emissions of water (electricity used to extract, convey, treat, and deliver water
- Embodied emissions of solid waste (life cycle emissions associated with solid waste)
- Embodied emissions of materials (emissions associated with the manufacture and transport of materials)

19. B: When a project team is ready to submit an application, it submits the applicable fee (based on project square footage) and required documentation. The project team may submit its application in two phases (review of design-related prerequisites and credits before construction and the construction-related credits upon project completion), or it may submit the application once (upon completion of the project). Credits are not granted until final review upon project completion.

20. A: The Credit Interpretation Request (CIR) and ruling process allows project applicants to seek technical and administrative guidance on how specific LEED credits apply to their project. The USGBC encourages project teams to review both the LEED Reference Guide and CIR pages of the website to see whether they can find the information they need before submitting a CIR.

21. A, B, & C: The most sustainable sites are those that reduce transportation demand, restore degraded or contaminated areas, minimize impact (such as light pollution), and manage water runoff to protect water quality and aquatic ecosystems. The fourth aspect is site selection.

22. A & C: Both a former gas station and a deserted building meet the restore ideal of restoring degraded or contaminated areas. The deserted building would likely be near public transportation, thereby reducing transportation demand. Sites that are not LEED preferred sites include the following:
- Sites on "prime farmland"
- Sites on previously undeveloped land where the elevation is lower than 5 feet above the 100-year flood
- Sites on land identified as habitat for threatened or endangered species
- Sites within 100 feet of wetlands
- Sites on previously undeveloped land within 50 feet of a water body
- Sites on land that prior to acquisition was a public park

23. B: The intentions of both MR Credit 5.1 – 10% Extracted, Processed & Manufactured Regionally and MR Credit 5.2 - 20% Extracted, Processed & Manufactured Regionally are to "increase the demand for building materials that have been extracted, processed, and manufactured within the region, thereby supporting the use of indigenous resources and reducing the environmental impacts of transportation." Transportation (truck, train, ship, or other vehicle) costs, emissions, and the accompanying pollution are reduced. Additionally, local and regional economies are supported. "Regionally" is defined as within 500 miles of the job site.

24. A, B, & D: Providing more free parking encourages single-person vehicles; therefore, it does not reduce transportation-related emissions. Other strategies that will reduce transportation include: providing fueling facilities and preferred parking for alternative fuel vehicles, providing preferred parking for carpool and vanpool, advertising ride boards, and limiting the number of parking spaces to the minimum required by the building code.

25. B, C, & D: Paying for gas will not encourage workers to use public transportation.

26. A, C, & D: Efforts are underway to improve vehicle fuel efficiency, reduce the carbon intensity of fuels, and develop vehicles that use alternative fuel. Recent research suggests, however, that these efforts alone may not be sufficient to meet greenhouse gas reduction goals without changes in land use. Land use is ultimately what drives transportation demand and urban sprawl; therefore, transportation demand is growing faster than vehicles and fuels can improve. Green building professionals can slow or reduce transportation demand by reducing the distance needed to travel between locations.

27. B & C: LEED for Neighborhood Development's encouragement of development within and near existing communities or public transportation is intended to move toward the goals of: reducing vehicle trips, reducing miles traveled, and supporting walking as a transportation choice. A measure of "smart location" is access to transportation services. LEED recognizes projects that have 50% or more of their dwelling unit entrances within ¼ mile of bus or streetcar stops or within ½ mile of bus, rail stations, ferries, or trams. The variation in distances is reflective of residents' willingness to walk further to reach certain types of transit.

28. D: This is the EPA's definition of brownfields. If contaminated, the land can be remediated and reused. Cleaning up and reinvesting in these properties takes development pressure off of greenfield (previously undeveloped sites) and improves and protects the environment. There are often tax incentives and property cost savings offered for developing brownfields.

29. B: Impervious materials are those that do not permit water to pass through and be absorbed by the earth below the paving material. These materials increase runoff and put pressure on storm water systems and also have the possibility for contaminates to enter the municipal water supply and aquatic ecosystems. Other sustainable landscape strategies include increasing pervious surfaces, planning water zones, and using mulch. Low Impact Development (LID) strives to implement strategies that address how water enters, is stored in, and leaves the site.

30. B & C: Impervious surfaces are those that inhibit the absorption of precipitation into the ground, thereby promoting runoff that can carry entrained pollutants into the municipal water supply and aquatic ecosystem. LEED encourages and recognizes planning, design, and operational practices that control stormwater and the quality of both surface and ground water.

31. A, C, & D: Strategies for stormwater management include:
    1) Minimizing impervious surfaces by increasing the area of permeable surfaces, using porous paving material and open grid pavers
    2) Controlling stormwater by directing runoff into dry ponds, rain gardens, bioswales, and other features designed to hold water and slow runoff
    3) Capturing rainwater for nonpotable use

Projects with larger footprints have greater, not fewer, pervious surfaces, and diverting runoff into oceans dumps pollutants into the aquatic ecosystem. Vegetated roofs and cisterns are often used to control stormwater.

32. C: The EPA identifies nonpoint source pollution as one of the biggest threats to surface water quality and aquatic ecosystems.

33. A, B, & C: Indoor water is the water that occupied buildings use daily to operate (toilets, showers, sinks, etc.). Outdoor water is the water use to irrigate. Process water is the water that is used in industrial processes and building systems (cooling towers, boilers, chillers, washing machines, dishwashers, etc.).

34. B: As the demand for potable water increases, so does wastewater, which thereby increases the pressure placed on treatment facilities. Untreated water can overflow and contaminate rivers, lakes, and other sources of potable water. The construction of additional water treatment plants is costly and does not solve the problem of controlled, ever-increasing demand. LEED encourages and recognizes efficiencies that significantly reduce the quantity of potable water used, while still meeting the needs of its systems and occupants.

35. A, B, & D: Non-potable water is defined as water that is not suitable for human consumption without being treated to meet or exceed the EPA's drinking water standards. Each day, the U.S. population withdraws an estimated 400 billion gallons of water from fresh water rivers, streams, and reservoirs to support residential, industrial, commercial, and recreational activities. This accounts for approximately one-fourth of the U.S. supply of fresh water. Nearly 65% of this water is then discharged to rivers, streams, and other water bodies after use and, sometimes, treatment. The U.S. extracts 3,700 gallons of water more per year than we return to the natural water system in order to recharge our water supply. Many of the activities for which potable water is used can be safely replaced with non-potable water.

36. C: Strained wastewater treatment facilities can overflow bacteria, toxic metals, and nitrogen into sources of potable water.

37. A, B, & D: Submetering allows commercial buildings' operational staff to track how much water is being used for plumbing fixtures and how well the fixtures are performing. It also alerts staff if problems arise in the system.

38. A, B, & D: Using non-potable water reduces indoor water use by using the appropriate water, such as captured rain water, gray water, or reclaimed water for non-human consumption usage, such as for flush fixtures. Installing submeters reduces indoor water use by enabling the meter to monitor indoor water systems, track consumption, and identify problems early. Installing efficient plumbing fixtures reduces indoor water use by replacing fixtures that use a lot of water with new, low-flow or no-flush fixtures and by installing new flush valves or flow restrictors to decrease the water use of existing fixtures.

39. B: Also available are composting toilets and non-water-using urinals. Composting toilets are dry plumbing fixtures that contain and treat human waste via microbiological processes. Non-water-using urinals use no water; instead the water flush is replaced by a specially designed trap that contains a layer of buoyant liquid that floats above the urine layer, blocking sewer gas and odors.

40. B: In addition to A, C, and D, another point that a project team should consider is irrigation efficiency. Baseline versus design considers the amount of water the design case conserves over the baseline case. The baseline case represents the Energy Policy Act of 1992 (EPAct 1992) flow and flush rates. Gallons per flush (gpf) record the amount of water used by a flush fixture each time it is flushed. The baseline flush rate for water closets is 1.6 gpf, for urinals 1.0 gpf. Gallons per minute refers to the amount of water used by flow fixtures per minute. Irrigation efficiency refers to the percentage of water delivered by irrigation equipment that is actually used for irrigation and is not evaporated or blown away or falls on hardscape.

41. C: Spray systems have an efficiency of 65%, while drip systems have a 90% efficiency.

42. B, C, & D: Irrigation is a significant component of a commercial building's water use; thus, it is an area where water can be conserved. Native and adapted species are no-to-low maintenance landscaping options. Drought-tolerant and xeriscape planting also provide viable landscape options. Xeriscaping is planting that reduces the need to irrigate.

43. D: Non-potable water is not suitable for human consumption, but it can be used indoors for flush fixtures and outdoors for irrigation.

44. A & D: Processed water is used for industrial processes and building systems that provide cool air and water for building operations. Projects teams should consider installing submetering systems on major water-using equipment to determine how much water is being used, where it is going, and where to focus conservation efforts.

45. B & C: Energy Star is the result of a joint program by the EPA and DOE that provides energy efficiency ratings for energy-consuming equipment, such as major appliances, office equipment, home electronics, lighting, and heating and cooling equipment. ASHRAE 90.1 2004 establishes minimum requirements for the energy-efficient design of buildings, except single family homes and multi-family residential units that are three or fewer stories abovegrade.

46. A: In addition to using energy-efficient equipment and materials, reducing demand for energy is the first step toward conserving it. Green buildings and neighborhoods can reduce the demand for energy by using buildings that both capture incident energy (i.e., sunlight, wind, geothermal) and take advantage of technological advances in construction systems and site-specific shading/cooling opportunities.

47. A & C: Strategies for decreasing energy demand include:
- Establishing design and energy goals. Setting targets, establishing performance indicators at the onset of a project, and then periodically verifying their achievement.
- Sizing the building appropriately. An oversized building creates costs and unnecessary energy demand.
- Using free energy. Orient the building to take advantage of natural ventilation, solar energy, and daylight.
- Insulating. Design the building envelope so that it is efficiently insulated against heating and cooling losses.
- Monitoring consumption. Use energy monitoring and feedback systems to encourage occupants to reduce energy demand.

48. C: The adjustment applies to all LEED for Homes credits, not just those related to Energy and Atmosphere. It accounts for the material and energy impacts of home construction and operation. Depending on its design, location, and occupants, a 100% increase in home area results in a 15–50% annual increase of energy use and a 40–90% increase in the use of materials.

49. B & C: Green building emphasizes an integral approach that addresses issues such as heating, cooling, lighting, refrigeration, conveyance, and safety through a whole building design. To achieve a green building, these factors must be considered in relationship to one another and as elements of the whole. Strategies include:

- Identifying passive design opportunities (choice B)
- Addressing the building envelope (choice C)
- Installing high performance mechanical systems, specifying high efficiency appliance and equipment [Energy Star, not E-Star (Choice A)]
- Using high efficiency infrastructure and achieving efficiencies of scale [i.e., there would be multiple buildings on the a single loop not run independently (choice D)]
- Using thermal storage
- Using energy simulation
- Monitoring and verifying performance

50. D: This requires that an energy model for the proposed design be made. The systems and design elements are then updated throughout the design process as changes are made to the baseline design." Comparison of the baseline design to the baseline building allows the design team to rate the building's energy performance and evaluate the relative costs and benefits of different energy strategies.

51. A, B, & D: Process energy is not subject to the LEED minimum performance requirements. Examples include: office equipment, escalators, kitchen cooking, laundry washing and drying, and lighting that is exempt from the lighting power allowance.

52. B: Examples of regulated energy include: lighting for interiors, parking garage, surface parking, facades, building grounds, HVAC, service water (domestic and space heating).

53. C: Chlorofluorocarbons (CFCs) are hydrocarbons that deplete the stratospheric ozone layer. Refrigerants like HCFCs have a significantly lower ODP than CFCs. The Montreal Protocol seeks to phase out all refrigerants with non-zero ODP. All chlorinated refrigerants, like CFCs and HCFCs, will be phased out by 2030. A building cannot attain LEED certification if it uses CFCs refrigerants.

54. A, B, & D: In addition to these choices, renewable energy is understood to be biomass, wave, and certain forms of hydropower. LEED distinguishes between on-site energy production and off-site purchased green power. On-site production usually involves a system that generates clean electricity, for example, by using wind mills or solar photovoltaic power. Off-site power can be purchased through the use of renewable energy certificates (RECs).

55. C & D: Building commissioning ensures that a building's systems perform according to the owner's requirements, BOD (i.e., the basis of design), and also the construction documents. There are times when the performance that is promised and anticipated in design is undermined by design flaws, construction defects, equipment malfunction, and deferred maintenance. Commissioning is a quality control strategy to detect and correct deficiencies. A building cannot attain LEED certification without fundamental commissioning.

56. A & C: Buildings generate a large amount waste throughout their life cycles (construction through demolition). The quantity of waste leaving the site can be reduced through smart purchasing choices and recycling programs. Materials and resource choices should focus on the health and productivity of the occupants, as well as the social, economic, and environmental impacts of the decisions made.

57. B: Other strategies include: rapidly-renewable materials (those that take less than 10 years—not 5—to grow or raise), recycled content, regional materials (materials that originate with 500 miles of the project site), reuse, sustainable forestry (FSC certified wood), and waste diversion.

58. C & D: The intent of LEED credits in Waste Management is to reduce the amount of waste and toxins hauled to landfills and incineration facilities. Recycling, reusing, and reducing during construction and daily operation of the building are encouraged.

59. A, B, & D: CFCs (Chlorofluorocarbons) are contained in refrigerants; they are not produced during decay. The EPA estimates that the U.S. currently recycles about 32% of its solid waste. It also estimates that increasing this recycling rate to 35% could save more than 5 million metric tons of carbon dioxide equivalent.

60. A, B, & D: FSC (Forest Stewardship Council Principles and Criteria) certification is given to wood products that meet the organization's standards to ensure that forestry practices are environmentally responsible, socially beneficial, and economically viable. Green Seal is an independent nonprofit organization that promotes the manufacture and sale of environmentally-responsible consumer goods. Green Label is administered by the Carpet and Rug Institute. The certification identifies carpets with very low volatile organic compound (VOC) emissions.

61. B: Regional materials are those that are manufactured, extracted, or processed within 500 miles of the project site. Therefore, only the percentage of glass in the windows counts toward points. Sustainable forestry products carry an FSC sticker.

62. A, C, & D: Rapidly-renewable materials are fiber or animal products that are grown or raised within 10 years and can be harvested in a sustainable fashion. Materials that should be considered include bamboo, wool, cotton insulation, agrifiber, linoleum, wheatboard, strawboard, and cork.

63. A & C: Reuse materials are those that are used in the same or related capacity as their original use. Salvaged, refurbished, or reused materials can count as points to earn this credit. However, mechanical, electrical, plumbing, and specialty items (such as elevators and equipment) cannot be included in the calculation of points.

64. A & C: Other resources for quantitative life cycle assessments (LCAs) include construction carbon calculator and EcoCalculator for assemblies. These rely on models and data-driven tools to analyze environmental aspects and potential impacts associated with products, processes, or services to provide an objective comparison of alternative design and construction practices.

65. C: Indoor environments can have significantly higher concentrations of pollutants than outdoor environments. New buildings have finish materials, such as laminates, carpets, furniture, paints, and stains that put out gas-volatile organic compounds (VOCs). LEED advocates providing stimulating and comfortable indoor environments that minimize the risk of building-related health problems.

66. A & D: Personnel costs, such as salaries and health care expenses, are larger than a typical building's operating costs. Thus, strategies that improve employee health and productivity, over the long run, are a net benefit to a company. Additionally, office space in green buildings commands a higher lease rate than office space in conventional buildings.

67. A & B: The University of California – Berkeley's Center for the Built Environment's studies have discovered that occupants of green buildings are significantly more satisfied with the indoor air quality of their building than occupants of conventional buildings. However, it has also been revealed that although green buildings often have superior air quality, they provide less satisfaction on measures of acoustic quality.

68. B & D: CO_2 builds up in spaces when there is inadequate ventilation.

69. A: Green Label Plus is an independent testing program administered by the Carpet and Rug Institute that identifies carpets with very low emissions of volatile organic compounds (VOCs).

70. B: MERV is the minimum efficiency reporting value. It is a rating that represents the efficiency of air filters in a mechanical system. Ratings range from 1 (very low) to 16 (very high). MERV ratings are reference in EQc3.1 and EQc5.

71. D: ASHRAE states that: "This standard specifies the combinations of indoor environment and personal factors that will produce thermal environmental conditions acceptable to 80% or more of the occupants within a space. The environmental factors addressed are temperature, thermal radiation, humidity, and air speed; the personal factors are those of activity and clothing." (ASHRAE)

72. A: ASHRAE states that: "The purpose of this standard is to specify minimum ventilation rates and indoor air quality that will be acceptable to human occupants and are intended to minimize the potential for adverse health effects. This standard considers chemical, physical, and biological contaminants that can affect air quality." (ASHRAE 62.1-2004)

73. A & C: Indoor environmental air quality can be contaminated by carbon dioxide; particulates; tobacco smoke; and off-gassing furniture, carpets, paints, adhesives, and cleaners. Outdoor air provides "fresh" air, which is beneficial for indoor environments. Paints carrying the GS-11 label are low-VOC products.

74. B & D: Increasing ventilation, coupled with using low emitting interior finishes that do not add pollutants to the indoor environment, will help control indoor contaminants. FSC-certified wood is a responsible forestry certification and does not relate to its indoor pollution potential.

75. C: Additional strategies include: monitor carbon dioxide, specify low-emitting materials, protect air quality during construction, conduct a flush-out, use an integrated pest management program, and provide adequate ventilation consistent with ASHRAE 62.

76. A, B, & D: Control over access to daylight and views, temperature, lighting, and acoustics not only increases an occupant's satisfaction with his or her space, but it has also been shown to increase human health and productivity.

77. B & C: Other strategies include: use daylight, install operable windows, give occupants ventilation control, give occupants lighting control, and conduct occupant surveys.

78. D: Color-corrected fluorescent lights are irrelevant to lighting control, so the other choices are effective ways to give occupants control over their personal lighting.

79. B & D: LEED ID credits are intended to encourage and reward projects and design teams that significantly exceed the minimum credit requirements and explore innovative green building strategies.

80. A, C, & D: A project team can earn exceptional performance credit by: doubling the density requirements for Sustainable Sites credits, significantly reducing indoor water use beyond the 40% required by LEED, significantly diverting construction waste beyond the 75% required by LEED, or providing more daylighting than the 75% required by LEED.

81. B & D: Collecting paper from shredders and installing more bike racks than required are not recognized as innovative strategies.

82. A: The project can earn only one credit for LEED AP involvement, regardless of the number of LEED APs on the project team.

83. B: The Montreal Protocol was opened for signatures in 1987 and entered into force in 1989. Since then, it has undergone seven revisions, and, if adhered to, the ozone layer is expected to recover by 2050.

84. A & D: RECs are renewable energy certificates purchased from a utility or a renewable energy provider. TRCs are tradable renewable certificates.

85. B & C: Vegetated roofs absorb and filter rainwater, thereby reducing the amount of water and "cleaning" the water leaving the site. Additionally, the installation of a high solar reflectance index (SRI) and/or vegetated roof reduces heat absorption and thereby the heat island effect.

86. B: "Smart location" examples are at least 50% of dwelling units within a ¼ mile walk of a bus or street car or ½ mile of a rapid transit, rail station, ferry, or tram terminal.

87. C: Low impact development programs comprise a set of strategies that address how water enters, is stored, and then leaves the site. LID minimizes impervious surfaces, protects soil, enhances native vegetation, and manages stormwater at its source.

88. A & C: A baseline versus design model comparison is used to determine the amount of water a design case conserves over the baseline design and to demonstrate the incremental improvement of a design building's energy performance over the baseline.

89. B & D: To be eligible for the LEED GA exam, an individual must provide a letter of attestation to verify one of the following: involvement in a LEED-registered project, current or previous employment in sustainable field, engagement in or completion of a program that addresses green building principles.

90. C: Only the actual percentage of post-consumer or pre-consumer content (by weight) of a product qualifies for LEED credit.

91. D: A COC certificate is awarded to companies that manufacture, process, and/or sell wood products that are made of certified woods and who meet FSC requirements.

92. C & D: The third category is Smart Location and Linkages.

93. B: The project administrator may appeal any ruling during the Construction Review. The project administrator will select the credits to be appealed; the responsible team member will add or change documentation as necessary, marking credits as complete when documentation has been sufficiently revised. Once appealed credits are marked complete, the project administrator may pay the appeal fee and initiate the Construction Appeal Review.

94. C: Credit compliance can only be submitted through LEED-Online. This data collection portal allows team members to upload information about the project and supplies credit templates to completed and signed by the specified team member.

95. D: Increasing footcandles increases illumination. Increasing the illumination of sites, in turn, disrupts the night sky and nocturnal animals.

96. B & D: High SRI surfaces enhance daytime illumination levels and reduce the heat island effect. Efficient irrigation systems that use gray water reduce the demand on municipalities' potable water resources. Increased building footprints and impervious surfaces do not absorb rainwater; therefore, they increase stormwater runoff.

97. C: LEED for New Construction addresses most commercial buildings and large (greater than four story) multi-family residential projects. LEED for Homes addresses single family and small (four or fewer stories) multi-family projects. LEED Core & Shell is for projects that require only the design and construction of the core and exterior shell. LEED for Multi-Family does not exist.

98. A: To qualify for a LEED credit point, a new building must either not use CFC-based refrigerants or, if reusing existing HVAC equipment, the project must complete a phase-out conversion prior to project completion.

99. B: Elements like roof and exterior wall construction; size, type ,and location of fenestrations; how the building is placed on a site; the building's the relationship to surrounding buildings; and how it is landscaped all affect the energy performance of a building.

100. A, B, & D: To achieve LEED certification, a project team must: fulfill all prerequisites, achieve a minimum of 40 points, register the project with the USGBC, and pay the appropriate fees.

Practice Test #2

Practice questions

1. Which of the following would disqualify a site from meeting the requirements of SS Credit 1 – Site Selection?
    a. The site is located on previously undeveloped land that is 10 feet above the 100- year flood level
    b. The site is located on previously undeveloped land that is within 100 feet of a water body
    c. The site is located on previously developed land that is defined as a brownfield by a federal government agency
    d. The site is located on prime farmland, as defined by the U.S. Department of Agriculture

2. Which of the following credits is NOT eligible for Exemplary Performance?
    a. SS Credit 7.2 – Heat Island Effect - Roof
    b. EA Credit 6 – Green Power
    c. IEQ Credit 5 – Indoor Chemical and Pollutant Source Control
    d. SS Credit 5.2 – Site Development – Maximize Open Space

3. Which of the following choices does NOT meet the requirements of SS Credit 2 – Development Density and Community Connectivity?
    a. The site is previously developed and is within ½ a mile of at least 10 basic services
    b. The site is previously developed and in a community with a minimum density of 60,000 net square feet per acre
    c. The site is previously developed and is within ½ a mile of a residential area with an average density of 10 net units per acre
    d. The site is previously undeveloped and is located within ½ a mile walking distance of an existing or planned and funded commuter rail, light rail, or subway station

4. You are an architect who is trying to determine whether your project meets the requirements of SS Credit 2. You conduct an assessment of the services located within ½ a mile of the project. Which three of the following services most directly count towards the ten that are required to meet Option 2 of this credit? (Choose 3)
    a. Public library
    b. Plumbing company
    c. 3-story office building housing an information technology company
    d. Thai restaurant
    e. Dry cleaners

5. Though building on an urban site has many potential benefits, there are some possible drawbacks as well. Which of the following is NOT a possible negative consequence of building on an urban site?
    a. Limited daylighting opportunities
    b. Undesirable air quality
    c. Existing utilities are already in place.
    d. Contaminated soils

6. Which of the following assessments is required for documentation regarding whether a site is contaminated under Option 1 of SS Credit 3 – Brownfield Redevelopment?
    a. ASTM E1903-97 Phase II Environmental Site Assessment
    b. EPA NPDES (National Pollutant Discharge Elimination System) – Phase I and II
    c. ASTM E1527-05 Phase I Environmental Site Assessment
    d. SARA (Superfund Amendments and Reauthorization Act) of 1991

7. Which of the following is a requirement for SS Credit 4.1 – Alternative Transportation – Public Transportation Access?
    a. Locate the project within ½ mile walking distance of one or more stops for two or more public, campus, or private bus lines usable by building occupants
    b. Provide a covered waiting area on the site that can shelter five percent of the building's FTEs for use as a public transportation stop
    c. Locate the project within ½ mile walking distance of an existing or planned and funded commuter rail, light rail, or subway station
    d. Locate the project within ¼ mile walking distance of one or more stops for one or more public, campus, or private bus lines usable by building occupants

8. Pursuing which three of the following credits could potentially reduce the size of a parking lot that is constructed as part of a project? (Choose 3)
    a. SS Credit 5.2 – Maximize Open Space
    b. SS Credit 4.1 – Alternative Transportation – Public Transportation Access
    c. MR Credit 2 – Construction Waste Management
    d. SS Credit 2 – Development Density and Community Connectivity
    e. SS Credit 5.1 – Site Development – Protect or Restore Habitat
    f. SS Credit 4.3 – Alternative Transportation – Low-Emitting and Fuel-Efficient Vehicles

9. How many bike racks are required if a building has 100 full-time employees and a transient population of 56, each of whom are in the building for an hour a day?
    a. 54 bike racks
    b. 3 bike racks
    c. 5 bike racks
    d. 6 bike racks

10. Which two of the following choices meet the definition of "preferred parking"? (Choose 2)
    a. Parking passes that are provided at a discounted price
    b. Parking spaces that are closest to the main access road into the site
    c. Parking spaces that are closest to the main entrance of the project
    d. Parking spaces that are designated for handicapped persons
    e. Designated drop-off zones at the building entrance for carpools and vanpools

11. In 2007 in the United States, what percentage of total greenhouse gas emissions was generated by the transportation sector?

    a. 8%

    b. 30%

    c. 57%

    d. 83%

12. Which of the following is NOT an example of a low-polluting, non-gasoline fuel for use in an alternative-fuel vehicle?

    a. Electricity

    b. Hydrogen

    c. Compressed Natural Gas

    d. Oxygen

    e. Ethanol

13. A project is attempting to get SS Credit 5.1 – Site Development – Protect or Restore Habitat. Because the site is a greenfield, the contractor working on the site must take which of the following actions in order to help obtain the credit?

    a. Plant fast-growing grasses to temporarily stabilize soils

    b. Limit all site disturbances to 40 feet beyond the building perimeter

    c. Restore or protect 50% of the site (excluding the building footprint) with native or adapted vegetation

    d. Perform a Phase I Environmental Assessment prior to beginning construction

14. Which of the following is least likely to be a benefit of incorporating a green roof into the design of a building?

    a. Can reduce the initial cost of the roof when compared to traditional EPDM roof construction

    b. Can potentially reduce heating and cooling loads on a building

    c. Can provide a habitat for birds and other wildlife to inhabit

    d. Can reduce stormwater runoff from the building

15. Having a green roof on a project would NOT aid in obtaining which of the following credits, assuming that the project is not pursuing SS Credit 2 – Development Density and Community Connectivity as well?

    a. SS Credit 7.2 – Heat Island Effect – Roof

    b. SS Credit 5.2 – Site Development – Maximize Open Space

    c. SS Credit 6.1 – Stormwater Design – Quantity Control

    d. SS Credit 6.2 – Stormwater Design – Quality Control

16. Which of the following is the minimum number of points needed to obtain a Gold certification using the LEED 2009 for New Construction?

    a. 60

    b. 70

    c. 79

    d. 40

17. Which three of the following choices are examples of impervious surfaces? (Choose 3)
    a. Concrete parking lot
    b. Gravel driveway
    c. Brick sidewalk
    d. Grass patio
    e. Asphalt road

18. Which one of the following is considered a nonstructural measure for stormwater management?
    a. Rain garden
    b. Rainwater cistern
    c. Pond
    d. Catch basin insert

19. Which of the following strategies does NOT help meet the requirements of SS Credit 7.1 – Heat Island Effect – Nonroof?
    a. Provide shade from the existing tree canopy or within five years of landscape installation
    b. Use hardscape materials with an SRI of at least 78
    c. Use an open-grid pavement system (at least 50% pervious)
    d. Provide shade from structures covered by solar panels that produce energy used to offset some nonrenewable resource use

20. Which of the following materials is most likely to have an SRI high enough to meet the requirements of SS Credit 7.2 – Heat Island Effect – Roof if it is used on a roof with a slope of 1:12?
    a. White EPDM
    b. Red clay tile
    c. Gray asphalt shingle
    d. Light gravel on built-up roof

21. Suppose an architect is helping to design a green roof. Which of the following would be the correct order to install the materials that form the green roof, with the material inside the building being first and the vegetation on top of the roof being last?
    a. Roof membrane, roof structure, drainage layer, soil, vegetation
    b. Roof structure, roof membrane, drainage layer, soil, vegetation
    c. Roof structure, roof membrane, soil, drainage layer, vegetation
    d. Drainage layer, roof membrane, roof structure, soil, vegetation

22. An architect is designing a building that is located within a national park. The project is attempting to obtain SS Credit 8 – Light Pollution Reduction. Which of the following zones would the project fall under for the purposes of exterior lighting levels?
    a. LZ1: Dark
    b. LZ2: Low
    c. LZ3: Medium
    d. LZ4: High

23. Suppose that a parking lot has an area of 100,000 square feet and contains 50 light fixtures mounted on poles throughout the parking lot. Each light fixture has a power of 200 Watts. What is the LPD (Lighting Power Density) across the entire parking lot?
  a. 2000 watts per square foot
  b. 0.002 watts per square foot
  c. 0.1 watts per square foot
  d. 1 watts per square foot

24. Which of the following professionals would be most likely to be a member of ASHRAE?
  a. Architect
  b. Contractor
  c. Mechanical engineer
  d. Lighting designer

25. All buildings attempting to be certified under LEED 2009 for New Construction must employ strategies that use what percent less water than the water use baseline calculated for the building?
  a. 10%
  b. There is no minimum required savings
  c. 30%
  d. 20%

26. Which of the following is a referenced standard of WE Prerequisite 1: Water Use Reduction?
  a. ANSI/ASHRAE/IESNA Standard 90.1-2007
  b. The Energy Policy Act (EPAct) of 1992
  c. ASTM E1980-01
  d. SCAQMD Rule 1168, Effective Jan 7, 2005

27. Which of the following fixtures is NOT counted when determining water savings for WE Prerequisite 1?
  a. Urinals
  b. Showers
  c. Kitchen sink faucets
  d. Commercial dishwashers

28. In order to obtain WE Credit 1 using Option 1, potable water consumption for irrigation must be reduced by 50%. Which of the following is NOT a suitable method for reducing potable water use?
  a. Increase in irrigation efficiency
  b. Use of captured rainwater
  c. Increase the density factor of the plants being used
  d. Use of recycled wastewater

29. How soon after installation must temporary irrigation systems be removed in order to comply with the requirements of WE Credit 1 – Water Efficient Landscaping?
  a. 1 year
  b. 6 months
  c. 2 years
  d. 3 years

30. How many points can a project obtain under LEED 2009 for New Construction if the water savings is calculated at 40%?
   a. 2 points
   b. 3 points
   c. 4 points
   d. 6 points

31. What is the intent of EA Prerequisite 3 – Fundamental Refrigerant Measurement?
   a. To provide HVAC systems that are more energy-efficient due to high performance refrigerant usage
   b. To reduce stratospheric ozone depletion
   c. To minimize direct contributions to climate change
   d. To minimize groundwater pollution by using nontoxic refrigerants

32. Which of the following protocols deals with the phasing out of CFCs and other ozone-depleting substances across the globe?
   a. Kyoto Protocol
   b. Geneva Protocol
   c. Montreal Protocol
   d. Stockholm Protocol

33. Which three of the following systems must undergo commissioning in order to meet the requirements of EA Prerequisite 1 – Fundamental Commissioning of Building Energy Systems? (Choose 3)
   a. HVAC systems
   b. Storm water collection systems
   c. Building envelope
   d. Lighting systems
   e. Domestic hot water systems
   f. Mass alarm notification systems

34. On a project that is greater than 50,000 square feet, which two of the following parties are allowed to act as the Commissioning Agent? (Choose 2)
   a. Employee or subcontractor of the general contractor with construction responsibilities
   b. Disinterested employee or subcontractor of general contractor or construction manager
   c. Employee or subcontractor, with construction responsibilities, of construction manager who holds constructor contracts
   d. Employee or subcontractor, with project design responsibilities, of the architect or engineer of record
   e. Owner's employee or staff member

35. Which of the following tasks is NOT the responsibility of the Commissioning Agent?
   a. Complete a summary commissioning report
   b. Review contractor submittals which are applicable to systems being commissioned
   c. Verify installation and performance of commissioned systems
   d. Write the OPR (Owner's Project Requirements) for the project

36. Which two of the following credits can most help contribute to the goals of EA Credit 1 – Optimize Energy Performance, if they are pursued? (Choose 2)
    a. SS Credit 7.2 – Heat Island Effect – Roof
    b. SS Credit 8 – Light Pollution Reduction
    c. EA Credit 2 – On-site Renewable Energy
    d. EA Credit 3 – Enhanced Commissioning
    e. SS Credit 4.3 – Low Emitting & Fuel Efficient Vehicles

37. A project is attempting to follow Option 2, Path 1 of EA Credit 1 – Optimize Energy Performance in order to obtain one point. This path involves following the ASHRAE Advanced Energy Design Guide for Small Office Buildings 2004. Which one of the following criteria must the building meet?
    a. Retail occupancy
    b. Use renewable energy sources for at least 5% of its energy
    c. Be less than 20,000 square feet
    d. Have an occupancy of fewer than 100 FTEs

38. Which of the following measures is least likely to result in significant energy savings in a building?
    a. Install daylight controls for all lighting fixtures near windows
    b. Install R-30, instead of R-10, insulation in the roof
    c. Use high-efficiency HVAC equipment
    d. Install glazing with a U factor of 1 instead of glazing with a U factor of 0.2

39. On which of the following types of savings are the thresholds for EA Credit 1 – Optimize Energy Performance – based?
    a. kWh savings
    b. Energy cost savings
    c. Percentage of energy that comes from renewable sources
    d. Percentage of energy generated on-site

40. What is the referenced standard for EA Credit 1 – Optimize Energy Performance?
    a. ASHRAE 55-2004
    b. IPMVP Volume III
    c. ANSI/BIFMA X7.1-2007
    d. ANSI/ASHRAE/IESNA Standard 90.1-2007

41. Which one of the following on-site renewable energy systems cannot be used to obtain points for EA Credit 2 – On-site Renewable Energy?
    a. Photovoltaic systems
    b. Geo-exchange systems
    c. Wind energy systems
    d. Solar thermal systems

42. Why are passive solar strategies not allowed to count toward EA Credit 2 – On-site Renewable Energy Systems?
   a. They do not save a significant amount of energy
   b. Enacting these strategies often requires the use of more building products which increases the amount of embodied energy in the building
   c. It is difficult to quantify the energy savings of these approaches
   d. The contributions of these strategies are reflected in other credits such as EA Credit 1

43. Which one of the following is NOT considered a passive energy-saving strategy?
   a. Installing sunshades
   b. Installing large amounts of thermal mass
   c. Installing high-performance glazing
   d. Installing high-efficiency HVAC equipment

44. In which state would a photovoltaic system most likely generate the most electricity over the course of a year?
   a. Arizona
   b. Oregon
   c. Florida
   d. Maryland

45. Which one of the following is a difference between Fundamental Building Commissioning and Enhanced Building Commissioning?
   a. The Commissioning Agent must verify the installation and performance of building systems for Enhanced Commissioning, but not for Fundamental Commissioning
   b. The Commissioning Agent must complete a summary report for Enhanced, but not for Fundamental, Commissioning
   c. The Commissioning Agent must review the Owner's Project Requirements and Basis of Design for Enhanced, but not for Fundamental Commissioning
   d. The Commissioning Agent must conduct a commissioning design review prior to mid-construction documents for Enhanced but not for Fundamental Commissioning

46. Which of the following methods is least likely to help a project achieve EA Credit 4 – Enhanced Refrigerant Management?
   a. Use only refrigerants containing CFCs in HVAC equipment
   b. Design a naturally ventilated building with no refrigerant based cooling systems
   c. Use only natural refrigerants in HVAC equipment
   d. Minimize refrigerant leakage out of HVAC equipment

47. Which of the following types of buildings uses the most energy per square foot, according to CBECS (Commercial Buildings Energy Consumption Survey) data?
   a. Warehouse
   b. Office
   c. Food sales
   d. Inpatient health care

48. If a project is pursuing MR Credit 1.1, which one of the following elements should NOT be included in the building reuse calculations?
  a. Exterior windows
  b. Roof decking
  c. Exterior skin
  d. Structural columns

49. A project is attempting to obtain MR Credit 1.1 – Building Reuse – Maintain Existing Walls, Floors, and Roof. If there is 100,000 square feet of applicable surface, how many square feet must be maintained and reused in order to meet the minimum threshold for one point?
  a. 35,000 square feet
  b. 50,000 square feet
  c. 55,000 square feet
  d. 70,000 square feet

50. Which of the following is NOT a crucial step in order to fulfill the requirements of MR Credit 2 – Construction Waste Management?
  a. Identify waste recycling companies in the area of the project
  b. Document the amount of waste that is taken to the landfill and the amount that is recycled and/or diverted
  c. Document the amount of waste that is incinerated rather than being taken to the landfill
  d. Meet with subcontractors to ensure they understand the requirements of this credit

51. Which three of the reasons below best explain why the recycling of construction waste debris is more feasible now than it was in the past? (Choose 3)
  a. New construction materials are less expensive than in the past
  b. It is now easier to obtain the raw materials to make construction materials
  c. Fees for dumping waste in landfills are higher now than in the past
   More companies are now involved in collecting recycling
  d. The process of manufacturing new construction materials has become much more energy-efficient over time
  e. Regulations for waste disposal have become stricter

52. A project is using materials that have been salvaged, refurbished, and reused in order to obtain points for MR Credit 3 – Materials Reuse. Which of the following materials would NOT be counted in the calculations for this credit?
  a. Wood planks from a demolished barn that are being used as flooring
  b. Ductwork that is leftover from an office renovation project that is being reused
  c. Brick from a demolished house that is being reused as cladding
  d. Pavers from a demolished house that are being reused as part of the hardscape around the building

53. There are several LEED credits that require knowing the total cost of construction materials for a project. If this information is not available, what is the best method to estimate the cost?
   a. Ask all of the subcontractors for a rough estimate of their material costs
   b. Multiply the total construction costs (including labor) for each of the relevant disciplines by 0.45
   c. Ask the owner for material costs
   d. Use the contractor's estimates from the bidding process

54. What is the process for determining the recycled content of a material for the purposes of MR Credit 4 – Recycled Content?
   a. Add the post-consumer and pre-consumer recycled content together
   b. Add the post-consumer plus ½ the pre-consumer recycled content together
   c. Add the pre-consumer plus ½ the post-consumer recycled content together
   d. Add the post-consumer plus twice the pre-consumer recycled content together

55. A project intends to include furniture in the calculations for MR Credit 4 – Recycled Content. Which one of the following credits does NOT require that the furniture be included if it is already being used for the above credit?
   a. MR Credit 2 – Construction Waste Management
   b. MR Credit 3 – Materials Reuse
   c. MR Credit 5 – Regional Materials
   d. MR Credit 7 – Certified Wood

56. What is the default value for recycled content that may be used for products made from steel?
   a. 90% pre-consumer
   b. 35% pre-consumer
   c. 25% post-consumer
   d. 80% post-consumer

57. A project site is located in Kansas City, Missouri. The architects have specified a particular type of gypsum board. From which of the following cities must this product be extracted and manufactured if it is to contribute to MR Credit 5 – Regional Materials?
   a. Wichita, Kansas – 200 miles away
   b. Denver, Colorado – 550 miles away
   c. Washington, DC – 1000 miles away
   d. All of the above
   e. Only A. and B

58. Which two of the following choices are the best reasons why regional materials should be used in a project? (Choose 2)
   a. Transportation costs are minimized when regional materials are used
   b. Regional materials are always less expensive
   c. Buying regional materials helps support the regional economy
   d. Regional materials are more durable
   e. Regional materials provide better aesthetics for a project

59. What is the threshold for a product or material to be considered rapidly renewable?
    a. It must come from a plant that is grown and harvested in one year or less
    b. It must come from a plant that is grown and harvested in two years or less
    c. It must come from a plant that is grown and harvested in five years or less
    d. It must come from a plant that is grown and harvested in ten years or less

60. Which three of the following resources are considered rapidly renewable? (Choose 3)
    a. Mahogany
    b. Oak
    c. Bamboo
    d. Cork
    e. Pine
    f. Straw

61. When pursuing MR Credit 7 – Certified Wood, a project must use FSC certified wood products. What does FSC stand for?
    a. Forestry Sustainability Council
    b. Forest Stewardship Council
    c. Forest Solutions Corporation
    d. Forestry Saving Council

62. What are the requirements to earn a point for MR Credit 7 – Certified Wood?
    a. Use 50% or more (by cost) of FSC-certified wood materials on a project
    b. Use 75% or more (by cost) of FSC-certified wood materials on a project
    c. Use 50% or more (by weight) of FSC-certified wood materials on a project
    d. Use 75% or more (by weight) of FSC-certified wood materials on a project

63. Which of the following choices is least likely to be the result of improving indoor air quality in a commercial building?
    a. Employees may miss fewer days of work due to illness
    b. Increased resale value of the building
    c. Decreased legal liability for the building's owner
    d. Reduced energy usage

64. Which of the following choices best describes the minimum requirement for EA Credit 6 – Green Power?
    a. Purchase 10% of electricity used annually from renewable sources
    b. Purchase 35% of electricity used annually from renewable sources for at least two years
    c. Purchase 50% of electricity used annually from renewable sources for at least one year
    d. Purchase 20% of electricity used annually from renewable sources for at least five years

65. Which of the following sources of electricity would be least likely to meet the requirements of EA Credit 6 – Green Power?
    a. Wind
    b. Solar electric
    c. Nuclear
    d. Biomass

66. Which two of the following requirements are prerequisites for LEED Certification? (Choose 2)
   a. Providing a dedicated area for the storage and collection of materials to be recycled
   b. If the building is new, demonstrating a 10% energy cost savings over a baseline case
   c. Recycling or salvaging 50% of construction waste
   d. Design HVAC systems to meet ASHRAE Standard 55-2004 – Thermal Environmental Conditions for Human Occupancy
   e. Ensure that all adhesives and sealants used inside the building meet SCAQMD Rule #1168 for VOC levels

67. Which of the following materials does NOT have to be recycled in order to meet the requirements of MR Prerequisite 1 – Storage and Collection of Recyclables?
   a. Paper
   b. Corrugated cardboard
   c. Metals
   d. Batteries

68. Which of the following actions related to indoor environmental quality must be taken as a prerequisite for a building to become LEED Certified?
   a. Permanent monitoring systems must be installed in order verify that the ventilation system meets minimum requirements
   b. The building must meet the minimum requirements of ASHRAE Standard 62.1-2007
   c. All adhesives and sealants used inside the building must comply with SCAQMD Rule #1168
   d. MERV 13 or higher filters must be installed in both the return and outside air ducts

69. What does the acronym ETS stand for when it relates to indoor environmental quality?
   a. Emitted Tobacco Standard
   b. Environmental Training System
   c. Environmental Tobacco Smoke
   d. Elevated Thermal Standard

70. IEQ Credit 1 – Outdoor Air Delivery Monitoring requires that monitoring equipment sets off an alarm when carbon dioxide levels rise too high. Why is this alarm requirement based on carbon dioxide levels?
   a. Carbon dioxide is harmful even if only present in slightly elevated levels
   b. High carbon dioxide levels indicate that a space is too cold
   c. High carbon dioxide levels indicate that the ventilation system is not functioning as designed
   d. High carbon dioxide levels could indicate that more outside air is entering the building through infiltration, and the building envelope should be tested for significant leaks

71. Complying with IEQ Credit 2 – Increased Ventilation is most likely to negatively affect compliance with which of the following credits?
   a. IEQ Credit 1 – Outdoor Air Delivery Monitoring
   b. IEQ Credit 7.1 – Thermal Comfort – Design
   c. EA Credit 4 – Enhanced Refrigerant Management
   d. EA Credit 1 – Optimize Energy Performance

72. A project is pursuing a comprehensive strategy related to improving the indoor air quality, both during and after construction. Which one of the following credits would help prevent new pollutants from entering the building once construction is completed?
    a. IEQ Credit 1 – Outdoor Air Delivery Monitoring
    b. IEQ Credit 3.1 – Construction Indoor Air Quality Management Plan – During Construction
    c. IEQ Credit 4.2 – Low Emitting Materials – Paints and Coatings
    d. IEQ Credit 5 – Indoor Chemical and Pollutant Source Control

73. IEQ Credit 3.2 – Construction Indoor Air Quality Management Plan – Before Occupancy?
    a. Perform a building flush-out prior to building occupancy
    b. Perform a building flush-out during building occupancy
    c. Perform air testing prior to building occupancy
    d. Perform air testing during building occupancy

74. Which of the following adhesives or sealants does NOT have to meet the requirements of IEQ Credit 4.1 – Low-Emitting Materials – Adhesives & Sealants?
    a. A carpet adhesive used on carpet in the office space of a building
    b. An adhesive used on ceramic tile in the bathrooms of a building
    c. A sealant that is used between concrete pavers in an outdoor courtyard
    d. Adhesive that is used to connect two metal panels in the lobby of a building

75. IEQ Credits 4.1 and 4.2 deal with the levels of which of the following compounds in products?
    a. VOC
    b. BTU
    c. DF
    d. dBA

76. Which of the following standards for paints and coatings is NOT referenced by IEQ Credit 4.2 – Low Emitting Materials – Paints & Coatings?
    a. GS-11
    b. GC-03
    c. SCAQMD Rule 1113
    d. SCAQMD Rule 1168

77. Which of the following choices is NOT a requirement of IEQ Credit 4.3 – Low-Emitting Materials – Flooring Systems?
    a. All carpet installed inside the building must meet the requirements of the Green Label Plus Program
    b. All carpet cushion installed inside the building must meet the requirements of the Green Label program
    c. All hard surface flooring inside the building must comply with the FloorScore Standard
    d. Unfinished floor areas inside the building must comply with the FloorScore Standard

78. Which of the following wood products does NOT have to comply with the requirements of IEQ Credit 4.4 – Low-Emitting Materials – Composite Wood and Agrifiber Products?
    a. Plywood sheathing
    b. Solid oak furniture
    c. Particleboard cores for metal panels
    d. MDF (medium density fiberboard) door cores

79. IEQ Credit 4.5 – Low Emitting Materials – Furniture & Furnishings counts as a credit under which of the following rating systems?
    a. LEED 2009 for New Construction
    b. LEED 2009 for Core & Shell
    c. LEED 2009 for Schools
    d. Choices A and C
    e. All of the above

80. Which three of the following products must meet the requirements of IEQ Credit 4.6 – Low Emitting Materials – Ceiling and Wall Systems when used inside of a school? (Choose 3)
    a. Gypsum board
    b. Light fixtures
    c. Artwork
    d. Insulation
    e. Acoustical ceiling tile
    f. HVAC ductwork

81. Which of the following must be installed at each regularly used exterior entrance in order to meet part of the requirement of IEQ Credit 5 – Indoor Chemical & Pollutant Source Control?
    a. A revolving door system
    b. An air curtain
    c. A permanently installed grate in the floor
    d. A vestibule

82. Which of the spaces below would need to be exhausted to meet the requirements of IEQ Credit 5 – Indoor Chemical & Pollutant Source Control? (Choose 2)
    a. Office
    b. Garage
    c. Cafeteria
    d. High volume printing room
    e. Lounge

83. Which two of the following techniques could result in a project requiring fewer overhead luminaries for general lighting? (Choose 2)
    a. Install task lights at every work station
    b. Minimize the glazing area around the exterior of the building
    c. Make the ceiling out of a material with a very low reflectance
    d. Build full height walls around every work station
    e. Make the ceiling out of a material with a very high reflectance

84. Task lighting must be provided for what percentage of building occupants in order to meet the requirements of IEQ Credit 6.1 – Controllability of Systems – Lighting?
   a. 50%
   b. 75%
   c. 90%
   d. 100%

85. Which of the following is NOT a condition for thermal comfort, as described in ASHRAE Standard 55-2004 – Thermal Environmental Conditions for Human Occupancy?
   a. Air temperature
   b. Outside dew point
   c. Air speed
   d. Humidity

86. Which of the following is considered a comfort factor that is taken into account by ASHRAE 55-2004 – Thermal Environmental Conditions for Human Occupancy?
   a. Type of clothing being worn by occupants
   b. Average age of occupants
   c. Average weight of occupants
   d. Density of building occupants in a building

87. A project is pursuing IEQ Credit 7.2 – Thermal Comfort – Verification and conducts a survey one year after occupancy. A plan for corrective action must be developed if what percentage of occupants is not satisfied with the thermal conditions in the building?
   a. 5%
   b. 25%
   c. 50%
   d. Both answers B and C
   e. This project cannot obtain this credit because the survey must be conducted within the first four months of occupancy

88. Which of the following is NOT a benefit of using daylight to help light a building?
   a. Glazing systems usually have lower insulation values than solid walls
   b. Using daylight can reduce lighting energy use when the system is properly designed
   c. Spaces with natural daylight tend to have increased occupant comfort
   d. Spaces with natural daylight tend to have increased occupant productivity

89. Which of the following buildings would provide the best opportunity for introducing daylighting?
   a. A four-story building with long and narrow floor plates in an urban setting
   b. A four-story building with long and narrow floor plates in a rural setting
   c. A three-story building with square floor plates in a rural setting
   d. A three-story building with square floor plates in an urban setting

90. Which of these factors most encourages mold growth?
   a. Moisture
   b. Food source
   c. Presence of mold spores
   d. All of the above

91. Which of the following can be used as the LEED AP for ID Credit 2 – LEED Accredited Professional?
    a. Architect at the design firm who is a LEED AP, but not working on the project going for LEED certification
    b. Architect at the design firm who is a LEED AP and is a principal member of the design team
    c. A LEED AP hired as a consultant for the project
    d. Choices B and C
    e. All of the above

92. What is the maximum amount of Regional Priority credits that a project can earn?
    a. 2
    b. 4
    c. 6
    d. 10

93. What organization administers the LEED credentialing exams?
    a. GBCI
    b. USGBC
    c. EPA
    d. ASHRAE

94. Which of the following is not an MPR (Minimum Project Requirement) for LEED 2009 for New Construction?
    a. The LEED project must contain a minimum of 1000 square feet
    b. The LEED project must serve 1 or more FTEs (Full Time Occupants)
    c. The LEED project must allow the USGBC access to energy and water usage data for at least five years
    d. The LEED project can be a mobile structure as long as it is not anticipated to move more than once in its lifetime

95. Registering a project with LEED-Online is important for which reason?
    a. The team receives a discount on certification fees if they register the project through LEED-Online
    b. Using LEED-Online provides instantaneous review of all credits when information is uploaded, therefore negating the need for Design Phase and Construction Phase reviews
    c. LEED-Online is the central location for managing all LEED documentation
    d. Projects that are registered with LEED-Online get review priority over those that are not registered

96. What is the best way to submit a CIR (Credit Interpretation Request)?
    a. Call the project reviewer at GBCI and explain the request to them
    b. Email the request to the project reviewer
    c. Submit the request through LEED Online
    d. All of the above are acceptable means of submitting CIRs

97. At which times must fees related to LEED be paid to GBCI?
    a. When the project is registered through LEED-Online
    b. When documents are submitted for the Design Review
    c. When documents are submitted for the Construction Review
    d. Choices A and B
    e. All of the above

98. Which of the following is NOT a category by which LEED credits are organized?
    a. Sustainable Sites
    b. Water Efficiency
    c. Materials and Resources
    d. Indoor Air Quality

99. When was the USGBC (United States Green Building Council) established?
    a. 1945
    b. 1976
    c. 1993
    d. 2005

100. Which of the following is most likely to be a benefit of employing green building practices on a project?
    a. Reduced operating costs
    b. Increased marketability
    c. Increased employee productivity
    d. Choices A and C
    e. All of the above

Answers and explanations

1. D: Answer A is incorrect because the threshold is 5'. B is incorrect because the threshold is 50 feet. Answer C is incorrect because part of the intent of this credit is to reduce the environmental impact of building. If a brownfield were chosen, this would improve the environmental condition of the site because it would have to be remediated prior to construction. D is the correct answer because building on this site would have a negative environmental impact on otherwise useful land.

2. C: All of the other credits have measurable objectives. For example, for SS Credit 7.2, 75% of the roof must be covered with materials with a certain SRI or higher. If 100% of the roof area contains a green roof, a credit for Exemplary Performance can be earned. The same is true for EA Credit 6 if a project gets 100%, rather than the 35% baseline, of its energy from renewable sources.

Also, a credit for Exemplary Performance for SS Credit 5.2 can be earned if the Open Space requirement for this credit is doubled. IEQ Credit 5 has no measurable objectives that can be exceeded, so no credit for Exemplary Performance can be earned.

3. D: A, B, and C all offer possible paths of compliance for this credit, although in and of themselves, they do not all guarantee that the requirements of SS Credit 2 are met. A site must meet the criteria of both choices A and C in order to earn the credit, or it must meet the criteria of B. D does not meet this credit because SS Credit 2 deals simply with the density of the built environment. There is a different credit that deals with proximity to public transportation - SS Credit 4.1.

4. A, D, and E: While choices B and C can be essential components in a mixed-use development, the intent of this credit is to channel development into urban areas and minimize the use of automobiles whenever possible.

A plumbing company would tend to not be the kind of business that someone would run to during a lunch break, for example, even though plumbing companies do provide valuable services. Having offices in a mixed-use development is also very important, but it is unlikely that this office will have people in the neighborhood walking there in order to conduct everyday business. The intent of this credit is to locate a building on a site that is close to services that its inhabitants can use every day to run errands.

5. C: All four of these choices are possible scenarios with urban sites, but C is the only choice that is a benefit and not a drawback. Daylighting opportunities can be limited by surrounding buildings, nearby industry or vehicle traffic could affect air quality, and previous development could have contaminated the soil.

However, having the existing utilities already running near the site saves time and money because it is less expensive to extend, rather than build, the utilities because less work is required on the part of the utility companies. It is true that having utilities in place could perhaps hinder the flexibility of the building layout slightly, but the benefit of not having to extend utilities far outweighs this negative.

6. A: Answer B is related to SS Prerequisite 1 – Construction Activity Pollution Prevention. Answer C is similar to answer A, but this assessment is used for SS Prerequisite 2 for Schools. A Phase I assessment does not involve collection of physical samples, whereas a Phase II assessment does. Answer D is much more general than the requirements of this credit.

7. C: A and D are incorrect because the criteria for Option 2, bus stop proximity is to locate the project within ¼ mile of one or more stops for two or more bus lines. Answer B is incorrect because, while it is useful to have a covered waiting area, this does not guarantee that there are any bus/light rail lines that go near the site. Also, the stops are not required to be on the site and can be up to ½ a mile away, depending on the type of public transportation.

8. A, B, and E: Answer A could minimize the size of the parking lot because it deals with the amount of vegetated open space on the site. The owner may want to minimize parking in order to maximize vegetated open space. The same is true for Case 2 of answer E. B is correct because having access to public transportation should reduce the number of people driving to the site, therefore reducing the amount of parking necessary. Answer C is unrelated to parking lot size. Answer D also does not concern parking lot size. Answer F has to do with number of parking spaces for low-emitting and fuel-efficient vehicles, not the total number of parking spaces.

9. D: First, one must determine the total number of FTEs. Each full-time employee counts as one FTE, and each transient counts as 1/8 of an FTE because they are there for 1/8 of the work day (one hour out of eight hours). Therefore the total number of FTEs for this building is 100 + 56/8 = 107 FTEs. Bike racks must be provided for 5% of FTEs, so 5% of 107 = 5.35. Since the number must round up, six bike racks are required.

10. A and C: B is incorrect because parking near the main access road into the site will usually maximize walking distance, not minimize it. D is incorrect because spaces that are reserved for handicapped parking may not be counted as preferred parking spaces per the definition of "preferred parking". E is incorrect because designated drop-off zones may be desirable, but this definition has to do with parking spaces, not zones where people are dropped off, which would in all likelihood be a no parking zone.

11. B: According to the LEED Reference Guide, "the transportation sector has generated more carbon dioxide emissions than any other end-use sector since 1999..." Residential, commercial, and industrial end-users are other prolific generators, with residential producing approximately 18%, commercial 19%, and industrial 35%, according to report DOE/EIA-0573(2008).

12. D: All of the other answers exemplify of low-polluting fuel sources. Electricity can be stored in batteries to power a vehicle. Hydrogen can be cleanly combusted in an engine. Compressed natural gas can be combusted in an engine and does produce greenhouse gases, but less than gasoline. Ethanol can be produced from crops and is therefore renewable.

In addition, for the purposes of LEED, efficient gas-electric hybrid vehicles are included as alternative-fuel vehicles. Oxygen is incorrect because it does not combust; it acts as an oxidizer to fuel other reactions.

13. B: A is incorrect because the strategy for controlling erosion and sedimentation has to do with Credit SS Prerequisite 1 – Construction Activity Pollution Prevention. C would only be applicable for

SS Credit 5.1 if the site was previously developed or graded. D has to do with SS Prerequisite 2 – Environmental Site Assessment for LEED for Schools.

There are other requirements for limiting site disturbance as well, so simply limiting disturbance to 40 feet beyond the building perimeter would not be enough to obtain this credit.

14. A: B is a benefit because the green roof can add insulating value to the roof and/or minimize roof temperatures. C is a benefit because a habitat for native wildlife can be created depending on the plants used. D is a benefit because the plants on the roof soak up rainwater, thus minimizing runoff. A is the correct answer because green roofs typically cost more to initially construct because the structure must often be increased in size and having more layers of material on the roof will naturally cost more to build.

15. B: A green roof would help obtain all of the other credits. A green roof helps meet the requirements for SS Credit 7.2, and it helps for SS Credits 6.1 and 6.2 because it both minimizes runoff and will typically remove pollutants from runoff as well.

However, a green roof will not help obtain SS Credit 5.2 if SS Credit 2 is not concurrently being pursued, according to the requirements of the credit.

16. A: The breakdown is: Certified – 40-49 points, Silver - 50-59 points, Gold – 60-79 points, Platinum – 80-110 points. 110 is the total number of points available in LEED 2009 for New Construction.

17. A, C, and E: Impervious surfaces do not allow water to penetrate through them and down into the subsurface. Instead water tends to run across the surface, which increases its velocity and causes erosion and sediment buildup when it leaves the impervious surface. Runoff often flows off of the site and then must be dealt with by municipal systems.

Concrete, brick, and asphalt are all impervious because they do not allow water through them. Gravel and grass are pervious because water can percolate through them and into the ground below. This minimizes runoff and recharges groundwater supplies.

18. A: The rain garden is considered non-structural because it allows stormwater to seep into the soil over time, as conditions permit. The construction of nonstructural controls is not as invasive as the construction of structural controls. These controls also tend to be less expensive to construct and maintain than structural controls.

The other controls are considered structural because they involve either a man-made device or a larger amount of construction. Structural measures are more effective at cleaning storm water in smaller amounts of space.

19. B: All of the other choices are viable strategies to obtain SS Credit 7.1, assuming that they are used individually or in combination over at least 50% of the site hardscape. B is not included in this list because an SRI of only 29 is required, not an SRI of 78. 78 is the value required for low-sloped roofs in credit SS 7.2.

An SRI of 29 would roughly correspond to gray concrete that isn't brand new, and an SRI of 78 would correspond to white concrete that isn't quite new, according to the reference guide. It would be difficult to keep the SRI of white concrete above 78 without constant cleaning.

20. A: Because the slope is 1:12, the roof qualifies as a low-sloped roof (slopes <= 2:12). Therefore, the required minimum SRI (Solar Reflectance Index) that must cover a minimum of 75% of the roof surface is 78. The SRI of white EPDM is approximately 84 and is therefore high enough to meet the requirements of the credit. Red clay tile has an SRI of about 36, gray asphalt shingle has an SRI of 22, and light gravel on a built-up roof has an SRI of 37, according to the reference guide.

If the roof slope were above 2:12, then red clay tile and light gravel would both meet the requirements because then an SRI of only 29 is required.

21. B: The roof structure sits inside the building envelope, and the roof membrane forms the last line of defense against water penetration. There could also be insulation on top of the roof membrane, but that was left out to simplify this example. Next would be the drainage layer that allows water that percolates through the soil to collect and be drained away, so that it does not sit on the roof and possibly make its way through the roof membrane. Additionally, if the water simply sits on the roof, it would be very heavy, which could be a structural issue. On top of the drainage layer sits the soil, and finally, the vegetation, which grows in the soil.

22. A: Sites in national parks, state parks, forest land, and rural areas fall under this category, which allows very little light to extend beyond the site boundary. The other categories allow progressively higher amounts of exterior lighting to extend beyond the site boundary because they each have progressively higher amounts of light surrounding them.

LZ2 sites are in residential zones, neighborhood business districts, and light industrial areas with limited nighttime use. LZ3 sites occur in typical commercial/industrial high-density residential areas, while LZ4 sites are found in high-activity commercial districts in major metropolitan areas.

23. C: In order to determine the LPD, one must divide the total number of watts of lighting power by the area of the site being considered. In this case, the total number of watts is the number of lighting fixtures multiplied by the number of watts per fixture. 50 light fixtures x 200 Watts per fixture equals 10,000 Watts. The site is 100,000 square feet, so 10,000 Watts divided by 100,000 square feet equals 0.1 watts per square foot.

24. C: ASHRAE is the American Society of Heating, Refrigeration, and Air Conditioning Engineers. According to the LEED Reference Manual, "ASHRAE advances the science of heating, ventilation, air conditioning, and refrigeration for the public's benefit through research, standards writing, continuing education, and publications."

While it is possible that the other professionals may be members of ASHRAE, it is most likely that a mechanical engineer would be a member because he or she would most often be dealing with HVAC and Refrigeration systems.

25. D: Under previous versions of LEED, there was no minimum required savings, but the 2009 version has enacted a minimum level of savings required for certification. According to the Reference Guide, "Efficiency measures can easily reduce water use in average commercial buildings by 30% or more." Therefore, a baseline of 20% should be an easily achievable standard.

Examples of easily implemented water saving features are low-flow toilets, sinks and showerheads, as well as the use of automatic on/off controls. Reducing water usage not only saves water, but also saves energy needed to pump water and heat it.

26. B: This act concerns energy and water usage in buildings and sets standards for their performance. Answer A is an energy standard that establishes minimum energy requirements for most buildings. Answer C is a referenced standard for SS Credit 7.2 – Heat Island Effect – Roof and includes how the SRI (Solar Reflectance Index) of a roof is calculated using its reflectivity and emissivity. Answer D sets the standard for VOC limits for adhesives and sealants.

27. D: Commercial dishwashers are not included in these calculations because they are not referenced in the Energy Policy Act (EPAct) of 1992. However, these types of devices (along with things like laundry machines) may be included in exemplary performance calculations for WE Credit 3. Urinals, showers, and kitchen sink faucets all must be included, though the reference guide notes that in some circumstances such as a kitchen sink faucet, low-flow fixtures may not be appropriate. This is because faucets may be used to fill pots and buckets and could dramatically slow the filling process, along with not saving any water.

28. C: Since more plants would be present, increasing the density factor of the plants used over a baseline case would increase the amount of water needed for irrigation. Lowering the density factor would save water for irrigation. All of the other methods are suitable for reducing potable water consumption. For Answer A, for example, drip irrigation may be used instead of sprinkler irrigation because it is significantly more efficient. For Answer B, rainwater can be captured on the roof or onsite and used to irrigate. Using this approach can also minimize and lower the volume of runoff that is released into stormwater systems.

Recycled wastewater (such as that from sinks and showers) can also be used for irrigation. This is called greywater. Water from toilets (blackwater) could potentially be used as well, though significant treatment would first be necessary.

29. A: A temporary irrigation system might be used if plants need extra watering in order to get established, but do not require any more water than is provided by natural climatic conditions after becoming so. Keep in mind that in some climates, it is not feasible to remove a temporary irrigation system after only a year because that is not long enough for some plants to become established. It is best to consult with an expert before deciding whether or not it is feasible to remove the irrigation system, or one runs the risk of the plants not taking hold and dying out.

30. C: A savings of 20% is a prerequisite and is therefore required for the project to become LEED Certified. A savings of 30% would earn 2 points, and 35% would earn 3 points. 6 points could potentially be earned if a project exhibited 50% water savings. This is because a credit for exemplary performance can be earned for 45% savings, and another credit can be earned for WE Credit 2 – Innovative Wastewater Technologies since potable water usage for building sewage conveyance will be reduced by 50%. Ordinarily, it should not be difficult to save upwards of 30% simply through the use of low-flow fixtures and automatic controls.

31. B: While some refrigerants are better than others due to their heat transfer potential, longevity, and environmental effects, the intent of this credit is to reduce ozone depletion by requiring zero use of CFC (chlorofluorocarbon) – based refrigerants in HVAC equipment. CFCs destroy ozone when

released into the atmosphere, therefore reducing the amount of protection that organisms have from harmful radiation. Choice C is incorrect because this choice is related to EA Credit 4.

This credit not only deals with refrigerants and ozone depletion, but also takes into account the global warming potential of refrigerants in terms of how much carbon dioxide they can add to the atmosphere. While nontoxic refrigerants are available for HVAC systems, this is not the intent of this credit.

32. C: The Montreal Protocol was enacted in 1989 in order to reverse ozone depletion. The Kyoto Protocol deals with stabilizing greenhouse gas emissions in order to minimize the effects of climate change on the Earth and was enacted in 2005. It has not been ratified by the United States thus far. The Geneva Protocol prohibits the use of chemical weapons and was enacted in 1928. There has been no Stockholm Protocol.

33. A, D, and E: The intent of this credit is to ensure that the major energy-using systems are commissioned, which is "the process of verifying and documenting that a building and all of its systems and assemblies are planned, designed, tested, operated, and maintained to meet the owner's project requirements," according to the reference guide. Ensuring that major building systems are designed, installed, and operating correctly helps reduce energy usage and system downtime, among other benefits.

As such, answers A, D, and E include the primary energy-using systems in a building and are among the systems that require commissioning. While it is, of course, beneficial to commission all building systems, these stand out above the others. Providing commissioning on other building systems is an approach that can, in some cases, help obtain a credit for Exemplary Performance.

34. B and E: These answers are correct because these parties do not have design interests in the project. Anyone who does not work on the design of the building, its building systems, or have a part in the construction process may be the Commissioning Agent. Anyone who has project design responsibilities or construction responsibilities may not be Commissioning Agent if the project is over 50,000 square feet.

However, if the project measures less than 50,000 square feet, parties with design or construction responsibilities may act as the commissioning agent. Any party that the owner chooses to be the Commissioning Agent is acceptable, again, as long as the party does not have design/construction responsibilities. Also keep in mind that the parties who may act as Commissioning Agent for obtaining the Enhanced Commissioning credit, differ slightly from those for the Prerequisite.

35. D: While choices A, B, and C must all be completed by the Commissioning Agent (CxA), it is the CxA's responsibility to review the OPR, but not to write it. This document, which outlines areas such as user and building requirements and energy and environmental goals, is to be used as a guide for the design team so they can ensure that their design is progressing towards the owner's expectations. The CxA and/or the project design team can help to write the OPR, but it is not a requirement. Ultimately, it is the responsibility of the owner to update this document.

36. A and B: These answers are correct because they directly correlate to lower energy usage when utilized in most climates. In order to obtain SS Credit 7.2, a lightly colored roof or green roof must be used. This can lead to lower energy usage for cooling because heat that would ordinarily be absorbed through the roof is reflected back into the atmosphere. SS Credit 8 minimizes the amount

of energy used for outdoor lighting, and reducing the amount of energy used for indoor lighting can help with this credit as well.

Choice C is incorrect because having on-site renewable energy does not, in and of itself, save on the overall energy usage of the building. It could however, reduce fossil fuel usage which is outside the scope of this credit. Choice D is incorrect because this credit can help ensure that the systems are functioning properly, thus saving energy. This is not taken into account, however, when conducting energy simulations or following prescriptive design paths. Answer E is incorrect because energy usage to vehicles is not covered by EA Credit 1.

37. C: In order to obtain this credit through this path, a building must contain office occupancy, and it must be less than 20,000 square feet. Because EA Credit 1 does not deal with renewable energy, just building energy savings, answer B is not applicable. While it is possible that a building that is less than 20,000 square feet would have an occupancy rate of less than 100 FTEs, the requirement deals with the size of the building, not the occupant load.

38. D: All of the other measures are likely to result in significant energy savings. Installing daylight controls saves lighting energy by automatically turning off lights when enough daylight is available. Installing insulation with a higher R value saves energy as well. High efficiency HVAC equipment uses less input energy to output the same amount of heating or cooling energy than low-efficiency equipment.

However, the higher the U Factor of a glazing system, the lower its insulation value. Glazing with a U Factor of 1 provides a much poorer insulator than glazing with a U Factor of 0.2. Therefore, using glazing with a higher U Factor will usually result in higher energy usage.

39. B: When calculating energy savings, the amount of energy saved must first be calculated. The units can vary. For example, electricity savings may be measured in kWh (kilowatt hours), while natural gas savings may be measured in therms. Once these values are known, the costs of each unit of energy must be used in order to determine total cost savings. When the energy savings is multiplied by the energy cost per unit, total energy cost savings can be found. This number must then be converted into a percentage based on the savings and the baseline usage.

Answer C deals with EA Credit 6 – Green Power, while Answer D may be applicable for EA Credit 2 – On-Site Renewable Energy, but only if the energy that is being generated on-site comes from renewable sources.

40. D: This answer is correct because this standard establishes minimum energy-efficiency requirements for buildings. ASHRAE 55-2004 deals with IEQ Credit 7.1 and 7.2 for Thermal Comfort Design and Verification and details the design conditions that HVAC systems must use.

IPMVP Volume III deals with techniques for measuring energy usage in buildings and systems once they have been constructed. This is related to EA Credit 5 – Measurement & Verification. ANSI/BIFMA X7.1-2007 deals with VOC limits in office furniture, which is related to IEQ Credit 4.5 – Low Emitting Materials – Furniture & Furnishings.

41. B: Photovoltaic systems convert sunlight into electricity, while wind energy systems harness the power of the wind to create electricity. Solar thermal systems use radiation from the sun in order to provide heat, often for hot water. Geo-exchange systems do not qualify as geothermal systems

because they do not use deep-earth heat. If a geothermal system that utilized deep-earth heat was used, this would qualify as an on-site renewable energy system as well.

42. D: With passive strategies, no renewable energy is being generated on-site; rather, it is being saved before it is even used. Therefore, these strategies count towards EA Credit 1 whose intent is to achieve increasing levels of energy performance. A is incorrect because significant amounts of energy can be saved if the strategies are correctly implemented. B is incorrect because passive strategies don't necessarily use any more or fewer materials than standard construction methods. C is incorrect because the energy savings can be quantified and are taken into account by the inputs that are required for calculations for EA Credit 1 – Optimize Energy Performance, depending on the compliance path that is taken.

43. D: Installing more efficient equipment is not a passive technique because energy (in the form of electricity or gas) is still being used to heat or cool the building. It is important to note that this approach can save large amounts of energy and is very effective, but it would not be considered a passive strategy.

All of the other choices are passive because once installed, they function without additional energy inputs. Installing sunshades can save energy because they can prevent the sun from heating up the space (reducing cooling energy needed) and/or they can act as a light shelf and reflect sunlight deeper into interior spaces. This could save on lighting energy. Using large amounts of thermal mass can minimize temperature swings in the building, thus saving heating and/or cooling energy. Due to its higher U Factor and other attributes, installing high-performance glazing can reduce heat gain in the summer and minimize heat loss in the winter.

44. A: Photovoltaic systems convert sunlight into electricity. Of the states above, only Arizona is located in a desert with warm temperatures and abundant sunshine year-round. Florida would likely have the second most amount of electricity generated, but there are more hours of the year that are cloudy than in Arizona. Less direct sunlight means less electricity generated.

The other states are both located further north, meaning that the sun is not as strong as in places further south. It is worth noting that electricity can still be generated when it is cloudy because solar radiation is still present, but the amount is significantly decreased from when the sun is shining at full strength.

45. D: Choices A, B, and C must be completed for both Fundamental and Enhanced Commissioning. They are all very basic and therefore must be done in order to ensure that the building is commissioned at even a minimum level. There are a few added responsibilities under Enhanced Commissioning, and conducting a check when the construction document phase is mid-way done is one of these. This helps to ensure that the design of the systems is progressing in a satisfactory manner and adds another opportunity for making changes if necessary.

Other additional tasks under Enhanced Commissioning are reviewing contractor submittals for commissioned systems, developing systems manuals, verifying that training requirements are completed, and reviewing building operation after substantial completion.

46. A: This is the strategy that is least likely to help with this credit. The intent of this credit is to reduce ozone depletion and minimize contributions to climate change. Therefore, refrigerants for HVAC equipment are judged based on their ozone depletion potential and global warming potential.

CFC's have both a high ozone depletion potential and global warming potential, and their use could make it difficult to achieve this credit.

Conversely, this credit is automatically achieved if no active cooling systems are used (Answer B). Regarding answer C, natural refrigerants tend to have a low ozone depletion potential and global warming potential. Because of the equation that is used to verify compliance with this credit, a low refrigerant leakage rate can help lower the final result of the calculations and help meet this credit. Therefore, choice D is also a good method to use for this credit.

47. C: According to Table 1 on page 329 of the reference guide, warehouses use 3.0 kWh per square foot per year on average. Offices use 11.7, inpatient health care uses 21.5, and food sales are significantly higher at 58.9. This range of numbers makes sense because warehouses have few occupants and are not likely to have stringent temperature ranges. Offices have a lot more equipment and people than warehouses, but health care facilities have equipment that is a lot more energy intensive. In addition, inpatient health care facilities are inhabited 24 hours a day, as opposed to offices which are usually only open less than half of the day. Food sales (i.e. grocery stores) use by far the most energy, mostly due to the large amounts of refrigeration equipment that must constantly run. These stores also use a lot of energy for lighting because they are a retail setting.

48. A: Each of the other materials must be counted because this credit deals with maintaining existing walls, floors, and roof, or the "bones" of the building. MR Credit 1.2 deals with maintaining and reusing interior nonstructural elements. Maintaining these elements cuts down on waste generated during the construction process, as well as the need for manufacturing of new elements, saving energy on both fronts.

One reason windows may not be included in these calculations is that new windows are often much more efficient than existing windows, especially if the building is older. Also note that structural columns are not explicitly included in the calculations; they are considered to be part of the walls, floors, and roofs that they support.

49. C: 55% of existing walls, floors, and roof must be maintained. 55,000 square feet divided by 100,000 square feet equals 55%. If less than 55% is maintained, no points will be earned. The thresholds for additional points are 75% for 2 points and 95% for 3 points for new construction projects.

These calculations include existing building structure, which incorporates the floor and roof and exterior skin, but not exterior windows and doors, or roof components that are nonstructural (such as insulation). Interior structural walls must be included as well, but not interior nonstructural walls, as those are included under MR Credit 1.2. In the case of interior structural walls, only one side of the wall is counted in the calculations.

50. C: This answer is correct because it is not a step in the construction waste management process. For the purposes of this credit, construction waste that is placed in a landfill is the same as construction waste that is incinerated. Waste that is incinerated does not count as being diverted from the waste stream because burning it can potentially have as many, if not more harmful, effects on the environment than burying it. Incinerated waste can introduce toxic chemicals into the environment, either through the burning process or by concentrating toxins in the remaining ash. This ash must then be disposed of somehow.

The intent of this credit is to divert waste materials so that they can be reused in other construction projects, which minimizes the need for creating new building materials. All of the other choices are obvious steps that must be taken in order to ensure compliance with the requirements of this credit.

51. C, D, and F: All of these are reasons that recycling has become more feasible. In the past, more room was available in landfills, so the fee to dump was lower. As space has become more limited, prices have increased. Additionally, in the past there were few companies that participated in the recycling process. However, as recycled materials have become more valuable, more companies have entered into the business. Finally, there are stricter limits on what can be taken to landfills or incinerated due to environmental concerns of what may happen to materials as they decompose.

Answers A, B and E are incorrect because if they were true (which they very well could be in some cases), this would probably lead to less, not more, recycling.

52. B: If ductwork is reused, it may not be counted in the calculations for this credit. Mechanical, electrical, and plumbing (MEP) components, along with items such as elevators, may not be counted because it is not advisable that these materials be reused in the first place. These systems are designed specifically for the applications in which they are installed. Reusing them could compromise the efficiency and safety of the new systems because of their technical complexity. All of the other choices could easily be reused because few modifications would be necessary, and these materials typically have quite a long lifespan.

53. B: If one does not have exact material costs, the fallback process is to multiply the total construction costs from MasterSpec sections 03-10 (along with the relevant sections of 31 and 32) by 0.45. This is a way of estimating the amount that is spent on materials. The remaining 55% of this number is roughly the cost of labor. Answer A is not correct because if one is asking the subcontractors for materials costs, one would want to get the exact numbers and not estimates. Otherwise this number is no more useful than the 45% estimate. C is incorrect because the owner usually has no idea of the cost breakdowns for the project, and it is not his/her responsibility to know. D is incorrect because these estimates can often vary greatly from the final costs of the project.

54. B: In order to determine the recycled content for this credit, one must determine the percentage of recycled material by weight. The recycled material may be pre-consumer, post-consumer, or a mixture of both. The LEED calculation involves multiplying the recycled percentage by the cost of the material. LEED only counts ½ of the pre-consumer recycled content in the calculation because pre-consumer recycled content is easier to obtain and more widespread.

Pre-consumer recycled materials are collected from the waste of the manufacturing process, while post-consumer recycled materials are those that have been used by consumers and discarded. It tends to be easier to recycle raw materials from the manufacturing process because they are still in their original state, as opposed to post-consumer recycled materials that have already been processed and used for their intended purposes.

55. A: If furniture and furnishings (products contained under Division 12 of the CSI Specifications) are included in the calculations for recycled content (because they may have a very high recycled content), they have to be included in the calculations for MR Credits 3-7 as well. Therefore, if the furniture is high in recycled content but does not count as a regional material and is not made from

certified wood, the project team may want to reconsider whether to include it in the calculations for recycled content. It may help the team gain one credit, but it might hinder getting two other credits. Detailed analysis would be necessary to ensure that the positives outweigh the negatives. MR Credit 2 – Construction Waste Management makes no mention of furniture as opposed to any other materials. It deals with construction waste that is recycled or reused, and waste from furniture counts as much as waste from any other source, though it is unlikely that the furniture installation will result in very much waste if it is manufactured in the factory.

56. C: If information is not available for the recycled content of a product made from steel, a default value of 25% post-consumer content may be used. The reason that these values may be used is that all new steel contains a significant percentage of recycled steel. Steel can be recycled over and over again with no ill effects to the steel itself and is quite easy to recycle when compared to manufacturing new steel. The steel in everything from cars to ovens can be melted down and turned into a steel column and vice versa.

With that in mind, it is beneficial to have actual recycled content information from the manufacturer because the recycled content is often much higher than 25% post-consumer. If the basic oxygen furnace process is used to manufacture steel, then the recycled content tends to be around 25%, but if the electric arc furnace process is used, the recycled content can be 80% or even higher. Steel is by far the most commonly recycled building product.

57. A: If products are to meet the requirements of MR Credit 5 – Regional Materials, they must be extracted, harvested, recovered, and manufactured within 500 miles of the project site. Wichita is the only city of the above choices within 500 miles of Kansas City, Missouri. It is important to remember that if only a certain percentage of a product is extracted, harvested, recovered, and manufactured within 500 miles of the project site, then only that amount may be counted for the purposes of this credit.

58. A and C: If a material is obtained from a nearby source, transportation costs will be minimized, though this does not guarantee that regional materials will be less expensive than a similar material from further away. In addition, buying regional materials pumps money directly into the economy of the region, rather than sending it to a different part of the country (or even to a different country). This aids both the manufacturing industry and the labor force of the area.

It is possible that in many cases regional materials could be more durable or could provide better aesthetics, but these choices are not always true and are, therefore, incorrect.

59. D: If a product comes from a plant that has a growing cycle of ten years, it is still much quicker than traditional wood products which may have a growing cycle upwards of 30 years or longer. In addition, in certain cases such as with plastic, plant-based products can replace petroleum-based products, thus reducing the usage of a nonrenewable product. In addition to taking less time to grow to maturity, rapidly renewable plant materials tend to require fewer resources to grow and have less impact on the environment during the growing process.

60. C, D, and F: Mahogany and oak are hardwoods, while pine is a soft wood. These trees take much longer than the required ten-year span to grow large enough to be harvested and are, therefore, not rapidly renewable. Bamboo grows quickly and can be harvested after two to seven years, depending on the species. Cork comes from the bark of the cork oak and can be harvested in slightly

less than ten years because the tree is not being cut down. Straw obviously has a short growing cycle and can be harvested every year.

61. B: FSC stands for Forest Stewardship Council. The FSC has established standards for the care and management of forests that ensure they are being managed in an ecologically-sound and sustainable manner. For example, FSC-certified forests do not cut down more timber than can grow back in a given year, and they take steps to minimize runoff that can degrade both the forest and its surroundings, among other things.

These safeguards will ensure that a certified forest can be run for many years without degradation of itself or the surrounding natural environment. The FSC also certifies organizations that can certify forest managers and/or companies that manufacture or sell wood products.

62. A: Of the total amount of money that is spent on wood products for a project, 50% or more must be spent on FSC-certified products. Examples of materials that would count toward this total are framing, blocking, sheathing (such as plywood), doors, wall or ceiling panels, and flooring, to name a few. If a product contains a mix of FSC-certified and non-certified sources, then the percentage that is certified counts toward the credit, while the percentage that is not certified does not count towards the credit.

Also note that recycled or reclaimed wood products do not count for this credit at all, so they may neither help nor hurt the project calculations.

63. D: Reduced energy usage is not likely to be a result of improving indoor air quality. In fact, improving indoor air quality is likely to use more energy. One method to improve indoor air quality is to raise ventilation rates (For example, see IEQ Credit 2 – Increased Ventilation). Pursuing this credit can result in higher energy use.

One reason is that more energy will be used for fans to increase ventilation, and increasing ventilation heightens the amount of conditioned air that is drawn out of the building. This air must be replaced, so more unconditioned air must then be brought into the building and heated or cooled appropriately. This needed additional heating or cooling uses energy. All of the other choices are definite benefits of increasing indoor air quality. Fewer health issues can increase employee productivity and result in a more pleasant work environment. A decreased chance of sick building syndrome also can reduce the owner's liability.

64. B: The building owner must enter into a renewable energy contract for a minimum of at least two years, and the energy must be certified as being renewable by the Center for Resource Solutions. The Center has a standard called Green-e that serves as a guarantee to the consumer that an energy source meets certain environmental standards.

Alternatively, if an energy source is not Green-e certified, it can be used if it is shown that it does meet the standards of Green-e certification. Note that a credit for Exemplary Performance is available if an owner purchases 100% of electricity from renewable sources for this same two-year period.

65. C: Nuclear power will not meet the requirements of Green-e certification because it is specifically prohibited by the Green-e standards. Even though nuclear power production releases very few emissions, there are environmental issues with the disposal of spent fuel rods and what

could occur in the case of a nuclear accident. Additionally, there are security concerns that are not present with other renewable sources of energy.

Wind and solar are the most obvious choices for renewable energy sources. Biomass electricity comes from burning plant matter, and obviously plants are renewable as well. A lot of biomass energy production comes from burning waste material that would have been otherwise thrown into a landfill.

66. A and B: MR Prerequisite 1 – Storage and Collection of Recyclables deals with providing space for recycling. EA Prerequisite 1 discusses required building energy savings. The other three choices deal with the requirements of other LEED credits, but these are all voluntary and not prerequisites. Recycling construction waste is part of MR Credit 2 – Construction Waste Management, ASHRAE Standard 55-2004 is part of IEQ Credit 7.1 – Thermal Comfort – Design, and SCAQMD Rule #1168 is part of IEQ Credit 4.1 – Low Emitting Materials – Adhesives & Sealants. If choices A and B are not accomplished, then a building cannot become LEED certified.

67. D: Though batteries can be recycled, it is not yet as common for them to be recycled as other materials because of the difficulty of recycling all of the different battery components. Additionally, batteries are probably not used as widely as the other materials which generate substantially more waste. It is required to recycle glass and plastics.

It is important to note that not all of these materials can be recycled in all locations at the current time. If a particular material cannot be recycled, space should be allotted for when recycling does become available in the future.

68. B: ASHRAE Standard 62.1-2007 deals with ventilation rates. Maintaining a minimum rate based on this standard is one step to ensuring that acceptable indoor air quality is maintained. In some cases, the local code may be even stricter than this standard, in which case, the local code must be used.

All of the other answers deal with other LEED IEQ credits, but none of them are prerequisites. Compliance with them is optional. Answer A deals with IEQ Credit 1 – Outdoor Air Delivery Monitoring. C applies to IEQ Credit 4.1 – Low Emitting Materials – Adhesives & Sealants. Answer D is part of the requirement for IEQ Credit 5 – Indoor Chemical & Pollutant Source Control.

69. C: ETS stands for Environmental Tobacco Smoke. ETS relates to IEQ Prerequisite 2 which prohibits smoking in buildings and within 25 feet of buildings. Smoking can be allowed indoors provided that strict separation from the rest of the spaces in the building is provided. Prohibiting smoking in the building allows the building's occupants to avoid the negative effects of secondhand smoke, and not allowing smoking near the building prevents ETS from being sucked in through the outdoor air intakes and contaminating the air that is being supplied to the building and its occupants.

70. C: Carbon dioxide is the gas that people exhale while breathing. If too much carbon dioxide builds up in a space, the most likely reason is that people are in the space and are breathing out carbon dioxide. If the levels are too high, this indicates that the ventilation system is not removing the carbon dioxide, and consequently the air in the space, quickly enough. If carbon dioxide is builds up, it is possible that other contaminants are building up as well, which can significantly degrade indoor air quality. Carbon dioxide in and of itself is not dangerous in elevated levels, but it

does mean that less oxygen can be present in a given space, which can reduce the comfort of occupants.

Answer B is incorrect because there is no correlation between temperature and carbon dioxide levels. D is incorrect because carbon dioxide levels are usually higher inside buildings than outside, unless a building is close to a major highway or other source of carbon dioxide. Even if a building lies close to a source, it is unlikely that enough carbon dioxide would enter via infiltration to set off the alarm.

71. D: Increasing the ventilation is most likely to reduce the possible energy savings because additional energy must be used to run the ventilation system, unless the building is naturally ventilated. More air must then be heated or cooled because a larger volume of air is being brought into the space. This takes additional energy. Increased ventilation goes hand in hand with IEQ Credit 1 because this credit simply ensures that the correct amount of outside air is being delivered. IEQ Credit 2 does not directly affect IEQ Credit 7.1, but does mean that more energy will probably be required to provide the temperatures that are called for as part of this credit. IEQ Credit is unrelated to EA Credit 4.

72. D: Answer A is incorrect because this credit deals with monitoring the flow rate of air into the building. It does not take into account pollutants that may be entering the building along with outdoor air. Answer B deals only with air quality during construction, not when the building is occupied. Answer C addresses paints and coatings that are installed during the construction process. D is the correct answer because IEQ Credit 5 requires the installation of entryway systems to minimize the pollutants that are brought into the building from the outside by a building's users.

This credit also requires that high-efficiency filters be installed in HVAC equipment to help clean pollutants from the air once they have entered the building.

73. D: This choice is not a method to fulfill the requirements of IEQ Credit 3.2. The requirements of this credit are very specific for each of the other options for fulfilling this credit. For example, if a building flush-out is performed prior to occupancy, the building must be flushed with 14,000 cubic feet of outdoor air per square foot of building area, and the air must have a temperature of at least 60°F and a relative humidity of 60% or lower. If building flush-out during occupancy is pursued, then air may be delivered at a slower rate so as to not disturb building occupants, but the same total volume of 14,000 cubic feet of air per square foot of building area must be delivered before the flush-out can be stopped. Finally, air testing can be performed prior to occupancy in order to ensure that key contaminant levels are within acceptable levels. If the levels are too high, a building flush-out is required. Air testing during occupancy is not allowed because building occupants could be exposed to high contaminant levels.

74. C: Credit IEQ 4.1 only governs adhesives and sealants that are used inside the building, defined as "inside of the weatherproofing system and applied on-site." Because choices A, B, and D are adhesives or sealants being used inside of the building, they must comply with SCAQMD Rule #1168 in order to meet the requirements of this credit. Sealant being used outdoors does not have to meet these same requirements because it is not releasing VOCs into the building.

With that being said, it is always good to use products with low VOCs outdoors as well, so that VOCs are not released into the atmosphere. Note that low VOC products do sometimes cost more and sometimes may not perform as well as products containing VOCs, though the quality of low VOC products is improving swiftly due to demand in the marketplace.

75. A: A VOC is a volatile organic compound that contributes to air pollution and can be harmful to humans when present in high levels. Some VOCs may even cause cancer, depending on exposure levels and duration. Benzene and formaldehyde are examples of VOCs. BTU stands for British Thermal Unit and is a unit of energy. DF stands for Daylight Factor which is the ratio of the amount of light available outside to the amount available in a given inside space. dBA stands for decibels which are used to measure sound levels.

76. D: SCAQMD is not a references standard for this credit, while each of the others is. Green Seal Standard GS-11 regulates VOC levels in paints and coatings that are applied to walls and ceilings. Green Seal Standard GC-03 regulates VOC levels in anti-corrosive and antirust paints. South Coast Air Quality Management District (SCAQMD) Rule 1113 regulates VOC levels for wood finishes and floor coatings, among other products. SCAQMD Rule 1168 regulates VOC levels in adhesives, sealants, and sealant primers. This standard is used in IEQ Credit 4.1, but not in IEQ Credit 4.2.

77. D: D is the only choice that is not a flooring system, and all flooring systems are covered by this credit. The Carpet and Rug Institute runs the Green Label and Green Label Plus programs, and the FloorScore standard covers hard flooring surface products such as vinyl, linoleum, and wood flooring, among others.

Unfinished flooring would typically be a concrete floor and could be a floor that is located in a service space such as mechanical and electrical rooms. This credit also requires that adhesives and sealants meet the VOC levels from SCAQMD Rule 1168, which is the standard used in IEQ Credit 4.1. If sealants or finishes are used on "unfinished" flooring as described above, they must still meet the VOC limits of SCAQMD Rule 1168.

78. B: This answer is correct for two reasons. For one reason, solid oak is not a composite wood or agrifiber product. Because it is not one of these products, it will not contain laminating adhesives which would contain added urea-formaldehyde resins. This credit prohibits added urea-formaldehyde resins.

Additionally, this credit deals only with base-building elements, and furniture is not considered a base-building element. Items that are considered FF & E (Fixtures, Furnishings, and Equipment) are not counted because they are not base-building elements.

79. C: This credit only counts under LEED 2009 for Schools. The requirements for this credit are to provide GREENGUARD certified furniture and seating or furniture and seating that off-gas below a certain level for various VOCs. Because children are more sensitive than adults to harmful chemicals, there is an additional credit available for furniture. Only furniture that has been manufactured a year or less prior to occupancy qualifies for this credit.

It is also important to note that while credits IEQ 4.1-4.6 are available for school projects to pursue, these projects may only earn a maximum of four points for these credits.

80. A, D, and E: This credit deals with materials that would be used in wall or ceiling systems. Gypsum board is the most commonly used wall material, and all building use (or should use) insulation. Acoustical ceiling tile is commonly used as well. These materials, along with all wall

coverings, must meet the requirements from the "California Department of Health Services Standard Practice for the Testing of VOC Emissions from Various Sources using Small-Scale Environmental Chambers."

While light fixtures, ductwork, and artwork could be part of the walls or ceilings, these systems would probably be very complicated to develop standards for because of the differences in these products from building to building.

81. C: A permanently installed grate that is at least ten feet long in the direction of travel would meet the requirement of this credit. A grille, slotted carpet system, or roll-up mat would meet the requirement as well. The intent is to catch dirt and pollutants from the shoes of the people that enter the building before they have a chance to enter the building and contaminate other spaces. Each of these systems can be cleaned more easily than a simple carpet system because they can be cleaned underneath where the contaminants have collected.

Choices A and B would be more useful in minimizing infiltration of cold or warm outdoor air into a building, and a vestibule could provide a place to have a permanent entryway system, but a vestibule by itself would not meet the requirements.

82. B and D: These spaces must be exhausted because they contain hazardous gases or chemicals. Garages contain potentially large amounts of vehicle exhaust, and high volume printing rooms contain high volumes of ink. Whether a printing room is classified as high volume or not is left to the project team, but any printers that are used for more than just convenience copying and printing should be classified as such.

The intent of this portion of the credit is to keep gases and chemicals from moving from one space in a building to another. This is accomplished by exhausting spaces with gases or chemicals, having the space enclosed with solid materials that go to the deck above or a hard ceiling, and installing self-closing doors. Typically, offices, cafeterias, and lounges would not contain hazardous gases or chemicals, so they would not need to meet these requirements.

83. A and E: A is correct because if a task light is available at every work station, there is less of a need to have enough ambient light in the entire space to conduct tasks. The light can be provided at the work surface rather than at the ceiling plane. E is correct because high reflectance materials reflect more of the light that sends them back into the space. Therefore, more light would be reflected off of a white surface than a black surface, and this reflected light helps light the space.

B is incorrect because minimizing the glazing area would either require more luminaries (because of less daylight) or in the best case, not change the number of luminaries needed. C is obviously incorrect because it is the opposite approach of Choice E, and D is incorrect because full height walls would prevent light from flowing throughout the spaces of the building.

84. C: Individual lighting controls must be provided for at least 90% of building occupants. Task lighting provides many benefits, so the intent of this credit is to extend those benefits to as many building-users as possible. The benefits include less need for overhead lighting and thus a possible energy savings, as well as more flexibility with lighting levels which can increase occupant comfort and productivity. Examples of task lighting include simple desktop lamps that are plugged into outlets and lamps that are hardwired into workstations.

85. B: All of the other factors are considered in ASHRAE Standard 55-2004 because they all play a role in the comfort of building occupants. One can consult a psychometric chart which shows how these factors are related. For example, in the summer a higher temperature with low humidity can be as comfortable as a lower temperature with higher humidity. Air speed can help cool the building occupants, but it can also be distracting and make tasks harder do to by blowing papers, etc.

The dew point outside should not affect the interior conditions. Rather, it is a factor that must be dealt with by the HVAC system when it brings in outside air in the course of conditioning the space. It should not affect the interior conditions unless a building is naturally ventilated or if it is well outside the normal range. Thermal radiation is also considered by this standard.

86. A: The type of clothing worn is important because it helps determine the clothing insulation factor in a building. If it is winter and people are wearing heavy sweaters, they will be comfortable with a lower temperature compared to people wearing shorts and t-shirts. Another human factor that is taken into account by this standard is the metabolic rate of the occupants. If it is a gym and all of the occupants are involved in physical activity, they will be comfortable with a lower temperature than people in an office.

The density of building occupants affects the design of the HVAC system, but this is a factor that the HVAC system must deal with; it does not affect the allowable comfort levels in the space. This standard also takes into account the building factors of air temperature, air speed, humidity, and thermal radiation.

87. D: If more than 20% of the building occupants are dissatisfied then a plan for corrective action must be developed. This plan must take into account the feedback received to ensure that problem areas are being targeted.

One reason that the threshold is 20%, as opposed to a lower percentage, is that the conditions for thermal comfort can vary from person to person, and it would be virtually impossible to please all occupants. In addition, people could answer survey questions negatively if they are unhappy with their job or because of other factors that are really unrelated to thermal comfort. 80% satisfaction demonstrates that the vast majority of building occupants are comfortable. E is incorrect because the survey must be conducted between six and 18 months of building occupancy.

88. A: Because glazing systems do usually have lower insulation values than solid walls, their use can result in higher energy usage to heat and cool the building. This may not always be the case, but materials with low insulating values let more heat pass through them than materials with higher values.

All of the other choices are benefits of daylight. Because light is already present, less electric light is needed (assuming the system works in conjunction with available light levels). Having daylight and views to the outdoors has been shown in many studies to increase occupant comfort and productivity.

89. B: A long and narrow floor plate works better than a square floor plate for daylighting because less space is located in the middle, far from the windows.

For example, if a building floor plate is 10,000 square feet, two possible options for its size would be 100 x100 (square) or 250 x 40 (long and narrow). If daylight can penetrate into the space 20' from each side, the entire narrow floor plate could theoretically be daylit, while only the outer 20' (or 64%) of the square plate could be daylit.

Daylighting will typically work better in a rural setting, or a setting without a lot of buildings nearby, because these buildings could block daylight from reaching the site at certain times of the day or year.

90. D: All three of these factors must be present in order for mold to grow. If one of the factors is taken away, then mold cannot grow. Obviously spores must be present for growth to occur, but this is virtually a given, as mold is almost always present in the air to some degree. Therefore, care must be taken to prevent moisture from entering a building. Also, mold uses organic materials as a food source, so the best ways to prevent mold growth are to use non-organic materials (such as glass mat gypsum board instead of paper-coating gypsum board, or metal studs instead of wood studs).

Proper detailing and placement of air, water, and vapor barriers in the exterior wall assembly can help mitigate problems with water penetration and facilitate drying of the wall cavity.

91. D: Anyone who is a LEED Accredited Professional (AP) and a principle member of the project team can be used as the LEED AP in order to obtain this credit. This includes architects, engineers, consultants, owners, and anyone else who is deeply involved in the project. People who complete the LEED accreditation exam with a passing score are considered LEED APs. Choice A is incorrect because this individual is not involved in the project and, therefore, has not had any input or impact on the project.

92. B: Regional Priority credits are new in LEED 2009 and are based on credits within the body of the LEED rating system. Six credits have been chosen for every zip code. They have been chosen because these credits are of higher relative importance in the area in question than perhaps other places in the country. For example, credits involving water savings might be regional priority credits in Arizona but not in the Pacific Northwest, because water is scarcer in Arizona. Places in the Pacific Northwest would have different Regional Priority credits.

A team does not have to do anything extra in order to earn Regional Priority credits. Instead, the credits act as extra credit for credits that have already been earned in the five credit categories. Again, note that though six credits are available, only a maximum of four may be earned.

93. A: The GBCI, or Green Building Certification Institute, administers these exams. The GBCI was created in January 2008 in order to provide an independent third party to manage the testing process. This was previously the responsibility of the USGBC (Unites States Green Building Council). This separation of the two entities helps reduce the chances of conflicts of interest arising and helps the program to meet ANSI standards.

Tests that GBCI administers are: the LEED Green Associate Exam and LEED AP exam. The credentialing maintenance program also ensures that LEED APs earn continuing education credits to maintain their knowledge base.

94. D: If a structure is mobile or designed to move even once, then it cannot qualify as a LEED project. The project must be designed for, constructed, and used on land in one permanent location.

Permanence is required because many credits are dependent on a building's location, and if the location were to change, then the new site would have different characteristics. Choices A and B set a minimum threshold for what constitutes a building that can be evaluated by the LEED rating system.

Below these thresholds, credits may not have the same relative value as they would on a larger building. LEED 2009 requires that the USGBC be allowed access to energy and water data so they may compare actual and calculated usages.

95. C: All projects must be registered and submitted through LEED-Online. Choice A is incorrect because no discount is given for registering for LEED-Online, as it is a requirement. However, projects that are registered by USGBC members do receive a discount. Choice B is correct because LEED-Online does not automatically review and approve the information uploaded for credits and prerequisites. It has checks built-in to ensure that data is entered correctly and that requirements are met, but it does not replace the Design and Construction reviews. Choice D is also incorrect because all projects must be registered with LEED-Online, so there is no priority for registering. Reviews can be expedited for an extra fee, however.

LEED-Online is the central repository of information for the LEED Documentation process. In addition to this, other general LEED-related information is available on the website.

96. C: Credit Interpretation Requests (CIR) must be submitted online, through the LEED-Online website. However, submitting a CIR should be a last resort. Other actions to take in order to resolve the question that requires the CIR are to call customer service, to examine the reference guide thoroughly, and/or to look online to see if the question has been answered by other CIRs that have already been issued. Once the CIR is submitted, all communications concerning that CIR will be electronic.

97. E: Fees must be submitted at all of these times. See the schedule of fees on GBCI's website for the most current information. Registration costs a flat fee for every project, while project certification rates for the design and construction reviews vary depending on the size of the building being certified. If the design and construction reviews are combined into one review, then it costs slightly less, and this fee is paid only once. Project reviews can be expedited for an additional fee.

98. D: Indoor Air Quality is not one of the environmental categories. The five categories are: Sustainable Sites, Water Efficiency, Materials & Resources, Indoor Environmental Quality, and Energy & Atmosphere. Indoor Environmental Quality is used as opposed to Indoor Air Quality because the credits in this category also deal with access to daylight and sound quality, factors which affect the indoor environment, but not necessarily the air.

Other categories in which credits may be obtained are: Innovation in Design for exemplary performance or innovative ideas, and Regional Priority for credits that have a higher importance in each geographic area.

99. C: The USGBC was established in 1993. When the USGBC realized that it needed a way to measure "greenness" of a building, it began to develop its rating system. The first version of LEED, LEED 1.0 was released in 1998. LEED 2.0 was released in 2000 with updates in 2002 in the form of version 2.1 and 2005 in the form of version 2.2. LEED version 3 is also known as LEED 2009.

LEED has expanded to cover many new sectors and building types. The current rating systems include: LEED for Core & Shell, LEED for new Construction, LEED for Schools, LEED for Neighborhood Development, LEED for Retail, LEED for Healthcare, LEED for Homes, and LEED for Commercial Interiors.

100. E: Each of these benefits is feasible when green building practices are employed. Reduced energy consumption can lead to lower operating costs. The buzz surrounding green building can increase the visibility of the project, and having a healthier environment indoors can help increase employee productivity and perhaps minimize sick-time taken by workers.

One possible drawback of green building practices is that they can add cost if not designed into the project from the beginning. Additionally, some components of the building may end up having a higher first cost, but this money can often be easily recouped through energy savings and gains in productivity.